ENDORSEMENTS

This book and Curt's wisdom have helped me grow in so many areas of my life and they will help you as well. Just take and apply these teachings and you will see transformation happen one day at a time.
—*TJ SMITH Co Founder Gym Growth Experts*

Using an athletic vernacular "No Strategy, No Victory" Curt Shows you how to turn life's defeats, into victories!
—*Nate Carr 3X National Champion & Olympian Bronze Medalist*

Every championship winning team has a playbook. Why would we expect anything different in our everyday life? Having gone through incredible wins and what some would call devastating losses, Curt does a magnificent job laying out the structure and formula to building out your own champion life playbook.
—*Rylee Meek Founder of Social Dynamic Selling & Kings Council*

Curt Tucker has drawn up an incredible playbook for you to live God's purpose for your life. He will not only motivate you but inspire you to live out your personal mission to be the champion God created you to be.

—*Andy Warren Lead Pastor Victory Church*

Curt's passion and enthusiasm for life & leadership is contagious. His book The Champion Life Playbook, will inspire you to take your life to the next level, and give you a proven playbook to help you get there fast.
—*Tim Goad Lead Pastor G5 Church*

Curt Tucker and his book The Champion Life have influenced me to not only become a 6-7 figure earner financially, but more importantly a better Husband, Father, and Leader.
—*Dustin Bower - Founder of Reputable Roofing and Remodeling*

THE CHAMPION LIFE
PLAYBOOK

THE
CHAMPION LIFE
PLAYBOOK

Your Game Plan to Creating a Life of
Abundance, Freedom, and Victory.

FOREWORD BY MIKE SLAUGHTER
CURT TUCKER

The Champion Life © **Copyright <<2022>> Curt Tucker**
All rights reserved. No part of this publication may be reproduced, distributed or transmitted in any form or by any means, including photocopying, recording, or other electronic or mechanical methods, without the prior written permission of the publisher, except in the case of brief quotations embodied in critical reviews and certain other noncommercial uses permitted by copyright law.

Although the author and publisher have made every effort to ensure that the information in this book was correct at press time, the author and publisher do not assume and hereby disclaim any liability to any party for any loss, damage, or disruption caused by errors or omissions, whether such errors or omissions result from negligence, accident, or any other cause.

Adherence to all applicable laws and regulations, including international, federal, state and local governing professional licensing, business practices, advertising, and all other aspects of doing business in the US, Canada or any other jurisdiction is the sole responsibility of the reader and consumer.

Neither the author nor the publisher assumes any responsibility or liability whatsoever on behalf of the consumer or reader of this material. Any perceived slight of any individual or organization is purely unintentional.

The resources in this book are provided for informational purposes only and should not be used to replace the specialized training and professional judgment of a health care or mental health care professional.

Neither the author nor the publisher can be held responsible for the use of the information provided within this book. Please always consult a trained professional before making any decision regarding treatment of yourself or others.

For more information, email support@curtdtucker.com
ISBN: 979-8-88759-153-7 (paperback)
ISBN: 979-8-88759-154-4 (ebook)

THIS BOOK IS DEDICATED TO:

My wife, Rachel, who has stayed by my side from day one, always believing in me, encouraging me, and challenging me to be the champion husband God created me to be. Thank you for always being you!

My kids, Mariah, Austin, Carson, and Carli, who inspire me to be a better dad and aren't afraid to challenge me. I am honored and blessed to be your Dad!

My Mentors, Mike Slaughter and Jay Meyer, who have gone before me, leading the way, teaching me what it means to be a Champion, and all the Awesome Men I have had the privilege to pay it forward to. You guys help me every day to raise my standards and keep me accountable to the call on my life. I am blessed to walk this journey called life with all of you. You know who you are!

CONTENTS

Foreword xi
Introduction xiii
Chapter 1: Let your Mess, Become your Message 1
Chapter 2: Building Your Champion Life on A Foundation of Faith 8
Chapter 3: Win Your Morning, Win Your Day 15
Chapter 4: Creating Your New Identity 37
Chapter 5: Being Fit For Your Mission 55
Chapter 6: Eating For Energy 66
Chapter 7: Recovery Matters 81
Chapter 8: My Battle with Mercury Poison 87
Chapter 9: Be the CE0 of your Family 97
Chapter 10: Raising Champion Adults 117
Chapter 11: Creating the right Money Mindset 124
Chapter 12: The Champion Life Challenge 147

FOREWORD

Curt and I have known each other for almost thirty years. I first met Curt when I was one of his baseball coaches in Jr. High baseball. We all knew Curt had an unstable home life. His dad was incarcerated for most of his growing-up years, so he lacked a healthy picture of what responsible adult leadership looked like. By high school, Curt fell into the wrong crowd and dropped out in his senior year.

The story of Curt's life is an amazing miracle! My wife Carolyn and I have been Curt and Rachel's spiritual parents for most of the last two decades. After dropping out of high school, Curt went on and worked for his GED. He is a loving husband and father who makes family his priority. I have witnessed Curt go from bankruptcy to building multiple successful businesses with his wife. Curt has gone from the bottom to experiencing radical life changes through his commitment to following in the steps of Jesus.

In the chapters ahead, Curt outlines the possibility of miracles in all our lives. Each chapter reveals in practical ways that miracles come with a cost that requires something from us. As Curt plainly states, "all leadership begins with self-leadership." God's miracles throughout both The Old and New Testaments reveal that miracles typically have two dimensions: divine intervention and human responsibility.

CURT TUCKER

The Champion Life Playbook hooked me in the first chapter with Curt's words: "If you want to impress people, tell them about your successes. If you want to empower them, talk about your messes!" I give thanks to God for this very practical step-by-step playbook!

Mike Slaughter

INTRODUCTION

Our lives are built by our days. **Every day, we get 86,400 seconds to choose what we want to do with those seconds;** how we choose to spend our time, either by investing it or wasting it, matters. Each day is an opportunity to create your Champion Life based on the decisions that you make with this time. How you think about yourself, how you think about your goals, and how you think about God's plan for your life. All this matters more than you think.

In this book, my plan is to give you a Game Plan for achieving a life filled with Abundance, Freedom, and Victory. What I like to refer to as the Champion Life! A life where you are winning in every area: Your Faith, Fitness, Family, Finances, and Fun!

In your Faith, having a personal relationship with God that is so freeing and truly knowing that we have a God that is for us, not against us. A Father who loves us and wants to see us win. Developing the kind of Faith that He desires us to have that allows us to Become the Champion leader he created us to be.

In your Fitness, where each day you have the mindset of a Champion, the emotional state of constant peace and joy, and a strong physical body that will allow you to do the things God has called you to do.

In your Family life, where you can have a marriage that is filled with Passion and Intimacy, living life with your best friend; creating a team mentality with your spouse and kids that sets you up to win as a family unit.

In your Finances, where you can earn the Income you desire, allowing you to do the things you want to do, when you want to do them, with whom you want to do them. **Money just makes you more of who you are**, and my desire is to help you earn more so you can give more. Give more to your family, give more to your church, and whatever else God puts on your heart. This starts with developing the right money mindset.

The last thing that I want to help you do is Have Fun! The Bible says, "A cheerful heart is good medicine!" Learning how to have fun and enjoy life is a must! So as we embark upon this journey together, my friend, can I encourage you to play full out? To read this book with the intention of applying the habits, rituals, and truths that I have learned in my life to yours with the expectation that your life can and will change for the better in one or multiple areas I have mentioned. That is my prayer for you. That this book would be a tool for you to use, to take your life to the next level, and allow you to experience Victory! 1 Corinthians 15:57 says, "But thanks be to God, who gives us victory through our Lord Jesus Christ."

I believe that when we realize the Power we have been given, the process of Victory has begun! I believe you and I were created to Win. We were created for a Purpose and a Reason, which I will talk about more in the coming chapters. So my friend, if you are ready to play full out in this game called life and experience what I like to call the "Champion life," Then keep reading. I believe you will be glad you did!

CHAPTER 1

LET YOUR MESS, BECOME YOUR MESSAGE

I want to let you know right off the bat here that I plan on being very transparent with you throughout this book. I have had so many great mentors in my life that I will tell you about in this book, and one of them is an incredible man by the name of Tim Goad. I remember him telling me one day. Curt, **If you want to impress people, tell them about your successes. If you want to empower them, tell them about your messes.** He encouraged me to be real, to let people know the truth. So that way, in helping men, I could give them what life is to a man's spirit, which is HOPE. See, I don't believe in failure as a negative. I believe in failure as feedback. I believe that the mistakes we have all made in life, if we choose, can serve us in so many ways. So yes, I have had my fair share of messes in my life that I now get the pleasure of sharing as my message. I would like to share a little of my story starting out here, so you can get to know who I am, what I am about, and what is most important to me. My hope is that through sharing my story, my messes, and successes, I will give you hope and encouragement to keep going and be inspired to create your Champion Life!

As I write this book, I am at the ripe young age of 40! It is hard for me to believe that I am 40 because I feel so young. I truly feel better today than I did in my early 20s. I'm sure it has a lot to do with the peace I have in my life. Peace, in my opinion, is more valuable than any amount of money I could ever be given. That peace is important to me because, for the first part of my life, it was non-existent.

See, I was born to a momma that had me when she was 18. She spent her entire senior year pregnant with me. My dad was in jail when I was born, and the early years were rough. All I remember of my early childhood was a lot of chaos. I don't feel compelled to share a lot about this part of my life in this particular book, maybe a future one, but I do want to share a couple of stories. See, I can remember being bounced around as a young kid from apartment to apartment. I remember living in my Grandma's dining room off the kitchen after we got kicked out of our apartment after my dad kicked in the door and beat my mom in front of me at seven years old, to then having to live with him a year later in a small trailer that daily I feared the rats from the cornfields, along with the fear of what mood my dad would be in, that day based upon his addiction to alcohol, which made him very angry most of the time. Looking back, I realize that these early years set me up to have many of the same problems in my early years as a dad. I look back on these days and think, how did I get through that? I know my dad loved me. He did encourage me to play football, be a hard worker, and do some good things. Those are the things I remember. Unfortunately, the memories of the struggle my mom, my little sister, and I had to go through carry more weight in my mind.

Today, I am actually grateful that my dad was the way he was because it is one of the things that has fueled me the most to be a loving and encouraging husband and father to my kids.

Some people are blessed to have an example of what to do, and some of us are given an example of what not to do. Either way, <u>it's our choice to make the best of what hand we are dealt. Everything in life really boils down to our choices.</u>

One of my core beliefs in life is that **<u>All leadership begins with Self-leadership</u>!** How you choose to lead yourself each day will have the greatest impact on how your life turns out. This is really the purpose of this book. My goal is to give you a practical Game Plan to lead your life with the best practices that I have found to produce the best results in my life that have allowed me to win. Many of us have given up because of something that has happened in the past, whether it was in our childhood, a failed marriage, a bankruptcy, etc... We have made the decision to stay stagnant, live in the past, and not go after the life God has for us.

See, I am glad that my childhood was the way that it was. I know that I'm not the only kid that had the wonderful experience of getting free lunch at school and getting made fun of, or having to go to the store and use the monopoly looking money, aka food stamps, to buy food, or having to wonder why we never got to go on vacation like everybody else. This was just part of the deal, the hand I was dealt that, to this day, drives me to do things differently than my parents did. My momma was an amazing woman, so I want to make that clear. She just never had a man of God in her life that wanted to play full out and give her the life she deserved. I was blessed to have the opportunity to take my momma with my family on a 7-night cruise in October of 2018 and let her experience what an incredible vacation looks like. We had an amazing time, going from island to island, enjoying some of the finest foods you can imagine, and just having an amazing time! Little did we know that just a month later, she would be diagnosed with lung cancer and be taken from us far too soon. This was a crushing loss to me, but all I could think about was how grateful I was that I had the opportunity to spend this time with her and pay her back for always doing the best she could and being a loving mom. She had such a huge heart and would always be in the mood to have a conversation and make you feel amazing!

One of the things my momma always encouraged me to do growing up was play baseball. Sports, for me, was an outlet. I was always playing some type of sport. Whether it was backyard football, playing basketball at the park, or home run derby at the ball fields, that was what would keep me out of trouble. My mom worked a second-shift job, leaving me a lot of freedom in the afternoon and evening to run. My stepdad, Tim, did his best to contain me, but I was a rebellious kid with a lot of hurt in his heart looking back. So, baseball was one of those things that I quickly found that I could excel at and fit in. It was also one of the things that allowed me to experience some normalcy as a young man, as I got to hang out with normal families, as I would like to call them, families that are much like mine today. One of the families I remember getting to hang out with was the Heinl family. The Dad, Rick, I always looked up to. He was a businessman, and his children included Rochelle, the oldest daughter who was in my grade, and two boys, Andy, with whom we played on the same baseball team, and Nick, the youngest brother. They lived in a beautiful home with land, took vacations as a family together, and were just a really cool family. I remember thinking, as I would go to their house, that one day I would have a nice house like theirs and be able to travel as they did. This was one of my first experiences of seeing what life could really be like getting a chance to hang out that summer and do life with the Heinl family.

That same summer, when I was 13, I was able to make a select baseball team, and one of the coaches was a man by the name of Mike Slaughter. He was the pastor of a local church called Ginghamsburg. Mike, Mr. Barhorst, and many of the other team dads became early mentors, men I looked up to; father figures if you will. Looking back, I know they loved me for who I was. They knew I had a rough life, but they loved me regardless. I was blessed to play on many of these teams because they were generous with their time and would give me rides, many times paying for my food after games and even my team fees each year. This is one reason why I believe we need more financial wealth, which I will talk more about later in this book. If they had only had enough for them, I would have never had the benefit of playing on these teams. There is a major reason why I am sharing this part of my story because this opportunity to play on this team is what really led me to give my life to Jesus 10 years later. I will share more in the next chapter as I talk more about my faith.

These summers that were filled with baseball were some of the best times of my life growing up. Being around these families and with these men. However, the summer was just that, the summer. Once summer was over, I would be back to not having many of these men in my life, lacking the leadership I needed, and not having it at my home. This led to many poor choices; hanging with the wrong crowds, alcohol, drugs, sex, and many other things. As those things began to fill my life more and more, baseball began to be less of a focus as high school went on, and eventually, I didn't care anymore. I believe my GPA was a whopping 1.3, and I never finished my senior year. **Here I was 17, a high school dropout, getting a GED, and wondering what my next step was in life.**

ADULTHOOD BEGINS

One failure after another took place after jumping from job to job. I finally landed a job selling cars at 19, which was a game changer. This would become my college if you will. In the next two years, I would learn how to sell, begin to read books like Think and Grow Rich by Napoleon Hill and learn how to really set goals. A whole new world had been opened up to me. I got to be around cool cars every day, hang out with people that had some money, and begin to dream again. What I found was something that I was passionate about. This was good for me professionally, but I still had the same old habits of drinking every night, hanging out at the bars on the weekend, and just living the playboy lifestyle. That was my life at 21, and then things changed. At that bar, The Brewery in Troy, Ohio, at the ripe age of 21, was where I met my Jesus-loving wife, Rachel. Neither of us was Jesus-loving at the time, more like two broken people in so many ways, looking for love in all the wrong places. I always said that I would never marry a woman who was older than me, who had been married before, or had kids, and that is exactly what happened. I am so glad today that God's plan is better than ours. Rachel and I began to date very quickly, actually the next night after meeting at that bar. Our first date consisted of smoking a joint and watching "Half Baked" together, laughing non-stop. Today we are blessed to do a lot of marriage coaching with couples, and when we tell them that was our first date, they don't believe us. Trust me when I say, God can change anybody. HE CAN! Rachel and I got married pretty quickly, and before I knew it, I went from being a 21-year-old bachelor to a 24-year-old with four kids in a short couple of years. The early years of our relationship were really built on lust, drugs, and just two people who didn't want to be alone. As our family grew, so did my need to drink, smoke weed, or escape on work trips to try to "find myself." This led to me making many poor decisions as I traveled down the road of infidelity, feelings of resentment, and, to be honest, hating the man in the mirror. I didn't know how to handle the life that I was living and the responsibilities that came along with it. Many of my days were filled with me drinking, controlled by frustration and anger, which led to abuse. All the things that I saw my dad do growing up that I said I would never do had now happened. What I put Rachel through in the early years of our marriage, still to this day, brings tears to my eyes. No person should have to go through what I put her through. My lack of leadership in our family eventually bankrupted us. Our home was foreclosed, both cars were repossessed, and we were living on government assistance. The silver lining to all this happening was that in this mess, I realized that I couldn't do life on my own and Rachel decided to go all in with Jesus. Her decision to follow Him at that time in our lives is why we are still married today, all these years later.

CHAPTER 2

BUILDING YOUR CHAMPION LIFE ON A FOUNDATION OF FAITH

There are two ways that I would like to define faith. First, the Bible says in Hebrews 11:1, "Now **FAITH** is being sure of what we hope for and certain of what we do not see. This is what the ancients were commended for. By faith, we understand that the universe was formed at God's command so that what is seen was not made out of what was visible." See, it is by it (faith) that we can have it (a personal relationship with God through Jesus Christ). I remember, in my early years, being so confused about how I could have a relationship with somebody I couldn't physically see. That is where faith comes in. Or what about: Is it possible to really restore my marriage after the damage I have done? Yes, it is, through faith and action! See, I believe that any goal is possible if you are willing to first have faith. Another word we could use here is belief! **<u>FAITH is the first thing we must have to even embark upon a new goal, dream, or desired outcome that we have for our life.</u>** If we don't think something is possible, the chances of us even getting started are slim to none. That is why it is important to fill our minds with the truth of the word. One of my favorite verses is Mark 9:23, which says that "all things are possible to those who believe."

See, when we believe, then we can proceed. We can get into action to make our desired outcome happen. The second thing we must do is have **FOCUS!** Once we have the faith to get going, next comes the ability to focus over a period of time to get the specific result we are looking for. I love the story in the Bible of Peter jumping out of the boat when Jesus called him. He did it! He actually walked on water! Why? How so? Because he was focused on Jesus. Then, as he began to take his focus off of Jesus, he began to sink. He left the one that gave him the power to do the supernatural, and he began to focus on the storm around him. I believe this happens to people all the time.

SOMETIMES YOU JUST HAVE TO GO!

I remember when Rachel and I went through the darkest points in our marriage early on after we had lost everything, and I truly thought it was over. I knew that I needed to change, and I knew that what I needed to do was turn to God. I just didn't know what that looked like. One of the things about me is that I like to know everything before I do anything. At least I used to be that way. Do you know what I mean? Every detail needs to be perfectly in place before saying "yes" or getting going. See that is the opposite of faith. So when I began to go to church, read the Bible every day and start praying, it was overwhelming. I didn't understand many of the things the pastor was preaching. I didn't understand many of the things I was reading in the Bible. I didn't understand how I could have a relationship with this guy named Jesus, who died on the cross and rose three days later. I didn't understand all that, but here is what I did understand. I understood that as I was doing the things I just mentioned, I began to feel different. I began to want to do better. I began to want to not be the man I had been for so long.

I will tell you the 100% honest truth. For the first three years, after I gave my life to Christ in 2006, I was still a hot mess. I was a transformation in progress. I later found out that there was actually a name for this. It's called "sanctification." **Sanctification is the process of being made new.** I often tell people that when you commit your life to Jesus, things don't magically get better, and all your problems go away, etc. No, many times, there is the potential that things will get worse. My mentor, Jay, actually told me multiple times that every time I was trying to go to the next level in my faith, I needed to double up on my prayers. See, there will be resistance when you are making the commitment to go to the next level, especially if it involves bringing people into the Kingdom of God with you.

MY SPIRITUAL FATHER ARRIVES

So as we began to grow in our faith, Rachel and I together, things weren't just all of a sudden amazing. There was still a struggle. The truth is we both had years of hurt, scars, trauma, bitterness, unforgiveness, and so many other things to let go of. Many years of bad habits, dependency on drugs and alcohol, and other self-destructive habits. The great thing was that we had put ourselves in an environment to win. **There is a saying that you will be the average of the five people you hang out with the most.** The church that we attended was led by a pastor named Mike Slaughter. Yes, the same Mike Slaughter that, ten years prior, was my baseball coach! See, when Rachel and I decided that we needed to find a church, the one that popped into my head was Ginghamsburg Church. It was a large church, so initially, we could hide in the back. At least for the first week or two, but once Mike, or as I call him today, "Poppy," saw me in church one week, the relationship that had started ten years prior had been reignited. He became more than just my pastor. He became my spiritual father; a man whose weekend sermon visits I looked forward to attending; a man I could look up to in all ways, as a man of God, husband, father, and leader. I would show up to church every Sunday, ready to learn. Slowly, one week at a time, my spirit was being renewed, things were beginning to change in me, and my faith was growing. What Mike was showing me was a different life. He got me to start believing that God really did love me; that he was for me and not against me; that even in the midst of all the wrong I had done and was still doing, Jesus loved me. It really wasn't about what I had done or didn't do, but what Jesus had already done. He became the first male role model I had ever had as an adult that I could follow and believe in. He made me want to do better. He was a man from whom I felt true love and grace, who loved me for who I was.

A STORY OF GRACE

I actually want to share with you a quick story about "grace" that was truly a defining moment in my life. In March of 2010, Rachel and I were beginning to have some success in business. Our marriage was starting to see some better days here and there. However, I still had some dark secrets that nobody knew about. One of those was the fact that we were still smoking marijuana every day. I remember leading a Men's Fitness Group at my church on Sunday nights and then going home after to smoke. "I need it," is what I told myself. I had done it for years, and it helped me cope with things that the enemy had me believing. I had tried to quit multiple times over the last three years but never seemed to be able to fully let it go. I believed wholeheartedly that the reason why my life had not gone to the next level was because of my dependency on this drug and not him. So after a couple months of things going wrong again in our marriage, business, and with our kids, it was impossible to ignore the signs God was showing me, so I made the decision.

At 5:24 am on March 15, 2010, I decided I was done smoking weed. Now, one thing I have learned in my life is that a decision without massive action is just a decision. **No change happens just by deciding. We have to put action behind that decision that forces change to happen.** So what did I do? I acted upon my decision. Here is where grace comes into this story. I knew that I needed to tell somebody about this secret that Rachel and I had. Nobody knew that we were still smoking weed. Here we were showing up to church every Sunday, serving in church, running a fitness business named Faith Driven Fitness, and so on. I knew that I needed to tell somebody to get this darkness out into the light. Now understand when I say that there was more darkness in our lives than just marijuana. Marijuana led me down other paths of dysfunction in our marriage, from sexual immorality, laziness and other things. So that morning, I decided to write Pastor Mike an email letting him know about the sin Rachel and I were living in. I can remember feeling so scared while writing that email letting him know the truth of what was really going on behind our four walls. What was crazy was that just a couple of weeks prior to this, Rachel and I were selected to be a part of a study group at his home. This was a huge opportunity as only about ten young couples in the church, the size of 3000, were selected, and now I am breaking this bombshell. So as I wrote the email, the fear, the worry, and other things set in. As I hit send, all I could think was, "This is the right thing to do."

That morning, I told my wife what I had done, and she was angry as a hornet at me. I had not only exposed myself but her as well. I remember awaiting the reply from Pastor Mike all day. "Was I going to get kicked out of the church?" "Was I going to be looked down upon?" "Surely we were not going to be allowed in the group." All these fears and worries were running through my mind. Really, what I was thinking was, "What have I done?" "How is this going to make things better?" Then I received an email back from Mike, which set me free. His response was filled with love and grace. This is how our Heavenly Father is, or in this case, my Spiritual Father. He let me know that he loved me and that he was praying for me. He encouraged me to take advantage of our church's counseling program. This led me to meet another successful businessman in the church who had struggled with the same things for years and was able to overcome them. Mike also let me know that my spot in his group was still available to us if we thought it would help us overcome and grow. WOW! I was blown away by the love, grace, and encouragement of his email. It was really at that point that I made the decision to go all in with my faith and let Jesus be the Lord of my life. Over the next couple of months, things would begin to happen that, to this day, are the foundation of the life I have today. A life filled with abundance, freedom, and victory in every area. I will tell you more about this in the coming chapters.

Over the last 12 years of my life, I can now look back and see so many times where my faith has been the foundation of all things good in my life. When you have strong faith and know that God is for you and that He wants you to win, I believe it creates a winning mindset that makes all things possible! Whether it's breaking free from an addiction, restoring a broken marriage, or starting a new business, it all starts with faith. Then, as you learn to focus on Jesus every day and the goal at hand, the only thing left is to follow through, knowing that every day, if you're willing to just keep going, **"keep doing the next right thing,"** as my mentor Jay says, things tend to work out. There is a saying that goes, "How tall can you build a skyscraper?" The answer is "as high as the foundation can withstand." I believe that when you are trying to build a Champion Life, one filled with victory in every area, your faith in God and in yourself will be the single most important thing that you can develop to ensure success that withstands. In this next chapter, I am going to share with you part of my morning routine and how I ensure that every day I am reinforcing the foundation of my life and building my faith to new levels. I believe this morning routine if you implement it, will be the single greatest gift I can give you to help you take your life to the next level.

CHAPTER 3

WIN YOUR MORNING, WIN YOUR DAY

As I said before, I am a true believer that our lives are built by our days. What we do every day matters. For years, I would just 'wake up and go." Actually, I would "wake up and react." React to whatever life was throwing at me or what was on my mind. Many times, when we wake up, the first thoughts that pop up in our heads are thoughts like, "I have to be at work by this time." "I have to take the kids here." "I need to pay that bill." This is what our minds are set on to begin the day. Many times it is scattered. Maybe you woke up late, hit the snooze a couple of times, and now you're behind. In a rush, you go, only to stub your toe, and now we let a big fat F bomb Go! Have you ever been there, my friend? I know I have a time or two!

Then the day came that I truly understood the power of MINDSET! See, It <u>is so important on a daily basis that you get your mindset, the direction of your focus set first thing in the morning</u>. Therefore, now we are not reacting to everything; instead, we are setting the environment for us to win. The best athletes in the world have developed a skill set in their specific sport that allows them to win because they have perfected their craft, and, literally, when they are in game mode, many times, they don't even have to think. They can just react. This is the goal you should have each day; to get so good at setting your mind in the right direction that reaching goals and having a life of abundance, freedom, and victory, aka The Champion Life, become automatic.

YOUR MINDSET IS LIKE A GPS

Think of your mindset as a GPS! When you are getting ready to go somewhere on vacation, and you're driving, the first thing you usually do before you leave the driveway is put the address into the GPS. This now becomes the direction that will get you there the fastest. That is why **I like to think of my mindset as my direction of focus!** This, along with my goals and the action steps I have set, almost guarantees that I will accomplish every goal I set. In a later chapter, we will cover my "WHY" Goal Achieving Process. Notice I called it the "Goal Achieving Process. Goal setting is important, but too many people set goals and don't accomplish them for many reasons. I am more about goal-achieving, and I am going to show you how to do this in a later chapter. For now, I want to focus on helping you win your day! As I go through the 10 Ways to Win Your Morning here, you will be setting yourself up to win every day and create your Champion Life. It is amazing what can happen when you're willing to invest one hour each morning into yourself. Remember, **the best investment you will ever make is in yourself.** When you create this discipline on a daily basis, everybody and everything around you gets better. I have included my top 10 in a one-page reference for you, and now I want to unpack all of them.

Building your Champion Life Morning
Curt Tucker

10 ways to WIN your morning, so you can WIN your day!

Prayer
The moment your alarm goes off, Thank God for the gift of today. Pray for his guidance and direction for the day.

Devotion
Take 5 minutes to read your Proverb of the day. The book of Proverbs was written by King Solomon, said to be the wisest man in the Bible. There are 31 chapters in Proverbs. Start your day with some great wisdom reading the chapter that goes along with the day of the month.

Journal
Take 5 minutes and write down a couple things that you feel can implement your devotion. Journaling is a powerful way to capture wisdom nuggets along with writing your goals down, etc.

Gratitude
Write down three things you are grateful for, and why you are grateful for them. Ex. I am grateful for my God who loves me even when I fail. Gratitude is the ultimate antidote for any negative emotion we feel. Choose to have an attitude of gratitude!

I am Statement
List 3 powerful I am Statements that you desire to be. Ex. I am a Loving Husband and Father. I am Healthy, Wealthy, and Wise. I am an extremely successful business man.

Meditate/Visualize
Take 10 deep breaths in your nose and hold for 5 seconds, and let it out focusing only on your breath and nothing else. This resets your nervous system. Then take a couple minutes to picture the things you want more of in your life. Close your eyes and picture the body you desire, the bank account you want, etc.

Goals
Write down or review your Top 3 personal and professional goals that you are working toward. Only 3% of people actually have their goals wrote down. Be part of the 3%!

Exercise
Do 10 -15 minutes of exercise. Weight training, running, yoga, etc. Anything to get your blood and oxygen flowing.

Eat for energy
Start your day off with a nutrient packed meal. I prefer a "Super shake". In mine I include protein powder, frozen avocado, blueberries, and a splash of unsweetened Vanilla almond milk.

Read 10 pages from a good book
Anything on Leadership, personal development, etc. Reading 10 pages a day/10 minutes sets you up to read approximately 18 books a year on avg. Leaders are Readers!

Faith   *Fitness*
CHAMPION BUILDERS ACADEMY
LIFE, LEADERSHIP, & BUSINESS COACHING
Family   *Finances*

YOUR HOUR OF POWER

So back to your mindset for now! How do we develop the right mindset that sets us up to win every day? We do it by taking control of the first hour of our day. No more waking up late, hitting the snooze button 97 times, and rushing through your morning. We do it by having a set morning routine that prepares us to be great for the day. In this chapter, I will lay out exactly what I do every morning that sets me up to win and be my best spiritually, mentally, and emotionally every day. As a fitness guy who has always worked out, I am a strong believer that we need to train the body every day, but in my opinion, it is even more important to train the mind and spirit. That is what this hour of power is all about!

So here we go! I am going to walk you through my morning and give you my exact routine to make it easy. I am a big fan of taking complex things and breaking them down to be simple so we can execute them. One of my core beliefs is that WE MUST TAKE ACTION! Knowledge is not power. Knowledge applied is power! Too many times, we overcomplicate things, and then we don't take action, which leaves us stuck. So I am going to make this super simple to execute, so you can crush your day!

RISE CHAMPION!

Rise at 5—Yes, for me, I choose to Rise Early. Why? Because when you are married with four kids and running multiple businesses, everybody is vying for your time and attention during the day, but at 5 AM, you have all the peace you need. I love this time in the morning! I sit my phone away from my bed so that I have to get out of bed to turn the alarm off.. This will eliminate you laying in bed and hitting snooze! **Then I head into the bathroom, look in the mirror with my hand on my heart, and say "GOOD MORNING CHAMPION." with a big smile!** I believe this is so important, friend. We have to learn how to love and encourage ourselves. We are creating a new identity here! We are building a champion, and it starts with the way we see ourselves, especially first thing in the morning when your subconscious is so impressionable. See, what you put into your mind first thing in the morning is so important. Some people wake up and watch the news. They fill their minds with all the latest garbage that happened the day before or allow somebody to set their focus for the day. I personally don't watch the news for this reason. Nowadays, you don't have to turn on the TV because everything is on your phone, right? That is why in the morning, a key part of this morning routine is that I don't turn my phone off airplane mode until my Hour of Power is complete. I don't want to break my focus, and you and I both know that as soon as we look at our phones, our focus will be overwhelmed with Facebook, emails, and who knows what else. So I say Good Morning, Champion, splash some cold water on my face, brush my teeth, and head downstairs to grab a cup of coffee to wake up the brain! Now I am ready to settle into my study for my HOUR OF POWER!

5:15 A:M:–PRAYER/DEVOTION/JOURNAL

PRAYER: The first thing that I do is pray. I love to just give God thanks for the blessings in my life, ask for forgiveness for anything that has popped up in my heart, and ask for wisdom for the day. I believe this is one of the greatest prayers that we can pray daily, that God would direct us, protect us, and yes, even correct us while giving us wisdom through the Holy Spirit each day that leads us each day to be our best. I love that in the Bible, Jesus' brother James tells us in James 1:5, "If any of you lacks wisdom, you should ask God, who gives generously without finding fault, and it will be given to you." **That excites me to know that I can pray for wisdom every day and that God wants to give it to me to help me win!** I can honestly say this is something that I ask for every day, and I am 100% certain it is a major reason why my life is so different today than it was ten years ago. I was trying to do everything on my own, which is why I failed repeatedly. Now I choose daily to ask God to fill me with his wisdom through the Holy Spirit and the Word of God, so I can live in a way that honors him each day.

DEVOTION- After I pray, I like to read from a devotional, or for me, many days, it is the Proverb of the day, or because I have been reading the Bible every day, I will just go to a part that I feel being called to read that morning. If you are new to this whole reading the bible thing daily, it's okay. Don't let this book overwhelm you. First of all, it is an amazing book. Many people have turned it into a religious book that people are afraid to read. The truth is, it's a fantastic book filled with so many great facts on how to live a Champion's Life. It is the most remarkable leadership book ever written, and as my wife says, it is our instruction manual. If you think about it, why is it named the Bible? I don't really know the answer. I'm sure I could Google it, but we choose to believe that it stands for Basic Instructions Before Leaving Earth! That is my story, and I'm sticking to it. All I can tell you is that when I started studying this book every day over 12 years ago, my life has never been the same since. I would encourage you to start by reading the gospels: Matthew, Mark, Luke, and John. Or keep it really simple if you're looking for some practical life wisdom, beginning with a Proverb a day. I really like this because there are 31 chapters in Proverbs and 31 days in a month. It takes about 2 minutes to read a chapter. The book of Proverbs has helped me in life in so many ways, friends! So I am going to share with you now one of my greatest hacks on how I learn, but more importantly, apply this wisdom to my life that ensures I get results. It is Journaling!

JOURNALING- Now, I use my journal for everything. It's where I keep my goals, notes from key meetings, and, most importantly, where I write down the things I am learning each morning. Remember what I said earlier? Knowledge isn't power. Knowledge applied is POWER! I like to say it like this. When we take INFORMATION and APPLICATION, we have TRANSFORMATION! So what I like to do is write in my journal about what I am studying that day, and I use the SON method that my Spiritual Poppa, Mike Slaughter, taught me. I have used this for years now, and it is powerful!

THE SON METHOD

Think of the SON method this way. Jesus is the SON of God!

S- Scripture

The first thing that I like to write at the top of my journal page is the scripture that I read that really stuck out to me that morning.

O- Observation

The O is for Observation, basically standing for my observation of what God is speaking to me that morning. As I am reading through scripture and a verse sticks out to me, I like to ask God, what are you trying to teach me here? It could be Curt.

You need to be more patient and less judgemental, give your kids more grace, believe in yourself, be confident, trust in me, love your wife, forgive that person, etc. Whatever I feel in my heart, whatever I am thinking in my mind, I like to write it down.

N- Name the Application

Then the last thing I like to do is write down how I am going to apply that day or in my life in general what I learned that morning. This is the most crucial part of this daily routine for me. This is where I take the direction God has given me and put it into action. It's amazing how, when we start doing things differently, we get different results.

This SON method provides me structure every morning to maximize my study time in the word and, most importantly, apply the teachings to my life!

5:45 A.M MEDITATION/VISUALIZATION/GRATITUDE

Meditation: I know there are many forms of meditation that people do, and some I believe in and some I really don't care for. What I will share with you is how I meditate and why I do it. In my opinion, the major benefit of meditation is that it allows us to slow down and focus. Now what you choose to focus on is the key. During my Hour of Power, the meditation that I like to do is just 5 minutes and flows directly into visualization, which I will go into more detail about next. My meditation begins with me closing my eyes while listening to some meditation music or waves crashing into the beach, which is my favorite. As I close my eyes, I begin to deep breathe in my nose and out my mouth for a good 4-second in, 2-second hold, and 4-second release. I like to focus on my breath for the first minute or 2, and then as I begin to feel calm, I ask the Holy Spirit, aka the living presence of God living in you and me, to clear my mind of any doubts, fears, or self-limiting beliefs, and renew it with the truth. Then I begin to think of the verses that align with the truth of God.

Romans 12:2 says, "Do not conform to the pattern of this world, but be transformed by the renewing of your mind." See what we choose to allow into our minds, and then focus on matters. **We can absolutely renew our minds by changing our FOCUS!** So let me give you an example here. Let's say you struggle with fear a lot. Maybe you find yourself constantly afraid that you are going to go broke, or that something is going to happen to your kids, or possibly a health issue. You can fill in the blank here on whatever it is that causes you to fear, which then leads to worry, which then leads to anxiety, which is basically us just worrying about a future outcome in our mind that hasn't even really taken place. It is a made-up story that we focus on so much that it literally changes our body chemistry and floods our body with cortisol, which is not good and really causes havoc in our lives and relationships. So the good news is I am going to share with you how to change that and go into more detail later. So in this situation with fear, if that is something that I was struggling with, a great verse that I would choose to meditate on would be 2 Timothy 1:7, which says, "That God didn't give us a spirit of fear, but of POWER, LOVE, and SELF-DISCIPLINE." Some interpretations even say, "SOUND MIND!" So now, instead of me living daily in fear, I have begun to live with the belief system that I am a person that has the POWER to do all things! When we live in fear, we tend not to take action. When you live in faith, and you believe you have the power to do anything, you tend to move into more of a massive action mode. This becomes powerful! So my form of meditation is to allow myself the time each morning to ask GOD to renew my mind and to focus on the things I need to do. Sometimes in the day, if I'm having one of those days, and I'm sure you know what I mean, I will take 5-10 minutes to meditate and do the same thing. This is a great way to reset your mindset, if you will, and create a sense of peace in your heart!

SEE IT, BELIEVE IT, AND ACHIEVE IT!

Visualization- Okay, now, after I have meditated, I begin to flow into about a 10-minute period of visualization. There is such power in visualization. Some of the top athletes and high performers in the world visualize on a daily basis. Growing up as a kid, I loved watching Michael Jordan play basketball. Michael would always talk about how he would visualize taking the winning shot and watching it go in before the game. At this time of visualization, I like to sit with my vision board in front of me. I have pictures all over it, representing all the things that are important to me in my life. I would highly recommend that you do this. There are books that you can buy that talk more about this in detail. One of the best ones out there is "The Complete Vision Board Kit" by John Assaraf. I have had multiple vision boards in my life. In the one I have currently, I kept it really simple and just took screenshots on my phone of things in my life that make me feel amazing, motivated, and inspired. Some are pictures of things I have already accomplished that remind me that I can do the things I have on my vision board that I want to accomplish. You can see my pictures representing many things, from my faith, generosity goals, family travel, beach home, reminders to raise my standards each day, and so on.

This is your vision board, so put whatever you want on it. I will look at this while walking on the treadmill during my morning workout at my house or on my phone if I'm at the gym. This is a powerful tool because **the Truth is you get more of what you focus on in life.** If you focus on all the negative things in your life, you will just get more of them. See, the brain really doesn't know the difference between if something is real or not when you close your eyes and begin imagining something. There are now thousands of brain scans with proof that when an athlete sits down, closes their eyes, and begins to visualize themselves playing the sport they play in their mind, those are the same things that they fire in the real game. Neurons, muscles, etc., are firing just by them sitting in a chair; visualizing. So, when you really understand how powerful this technique can be, it is something that you will absolutely make time for every day. See, most people will not sit down for 10 minutes to visualize because they think that would be a waste of time. However, I have learned that this is one of the best uses of my time each day because it trains my brain to focus on the things in my life that can help me get to my goals the quickest.

Many of us are in a hurry each day, and there are things all around us that could ultimately help us achieve our goals that we don't even notice. I was talking to one of my coaching clients a couple of weeks ago, and he was asking me about how I thought he should go about finding the right woman. He has had a couple of failed marriages in the past, and just the thought of dating again is scary to him. I began to ask him, "Well, do you know what you want?" He replied, "What do you mean?" I said, "Well, I think the first thing you need to decide upon is what exactly you are looking for in a woman. Like, what are the qualities that are important to you? Do you want her to love Jesus as you do? Do you want her to be into fitness like you are? Do you want her to like to travel as you do? "I then continued by saying, "I believe these things are important because you could run into this woman tomorrow at the store, and you wouldn't even know she was the one because you don't know what you're looking for. If you struck up a conversation with her, and you began to talk, ask questions, etc., you would know if you should move forward or not by asking her out for dinner or a cup of coffee. "

YOU ARE THE MAIN CHARACTER IN YOUR OWN MOVIE

So, visualizing, my friends, is really just a time where you can close your eyes and, on the movie screen of your mind, as I like to say, see the movie you want to live out in your life. See, you are the main character of your own movie. **Each day you are directing your life, living it out, and it is either giving you a sense of fulfillment or not.** So I am choosing to see what I want in my life, not what I don't want. I want to see it, feel it, and even touch it! The more you do this, the more it begins to feel real. You will notice that your thoughts change, your actions change, and, ultimately, your results change. I love to visualize earning more income and the tithe check I am going to write and all the people that money will bless. I love to visualize taking my family on an exotic vacation and seeing us all on the beach during the day, and enjoying dinner together at night! I love to visualize the home on the beach that I am going to live in and have people over to let them see what is possible. All these things make me feel good and get me focused on the things that are important to me each day. As I am wrapping up my visualization, the last thing that I do is give thanks to God for these goals coming to fruition, and I pray that His will be done. See, I believe we need to give God thanks in advance for what He is trying to do in our lives. Once I set a goal, and I truly believe that God is calling me in that direction, I am ALL IN! I am casting away any doubt, indecision, etc., and moving forward with massive action until completion.

THE POWER OF GOD'S WORD

One of my favorite scriptures is Mark 11:22–24. I will share it with you and then unpack it for you. I believe if you let what I'm about to unpack for you get deep into your heart, these verses can and will absolutely change your life. This passage has been a game changer for me and has helped me, along with the Holy Spirit, in setting so many people free. It says, "[22] Have faith in God," Jesus answered. "'[23] Truly I tell you, if anyone says to this mountain, Go, throw yourself into the sea, and does not doubt in their heart but believes that what they say will happen, it will be done for them. ²⁴ Therefore, **I tell you, whatever you ask for in prayer, believe that you have received it, and it will be yours!**" Man, those verses are powerful! I want you to read those verses again right now before you move on and read them, knowing that this is God's truth. These are the words of Jesus, not Curt Tucker.

Now I will share with you what I believe Jesus is saying or how I interpret these verses. I will start by saying that I believe that we can ask God for anything. I believe that we serve a God who is limitless. I believe God is a Father who loves his children no matter what. I believe that if I ask for something and it's not for me, then he won't give it to me. I also believe that we should ask for things and pray in a way that is not self-centered, but that is more focused on the fruitfulness of God's kingdom. Let's check this out, though. Let's unpack these verses above. First, Jesus was talking to his disciples about a fig tree that had withered and that Jesus had cursed. As he began to teach them, here is what I took away from these verses. Let me start with verse 23. Jesus says, "if anyone says to this mountain, GO, throw yourself into the sea," and does not doubt in their heart but believes that what they say will happen, it will be done for them. My first question to you is: What is your mountain? What is the one thing standing in your way right now from you living the champion life that God has created you to live? Is it an addiction? A certain drug, alcohol, or pornography. All these things create havoc and make it pretty much impossible to have healthy relationships and a great marriage. They leave you living a life of guilt and shame each day. What about your fear of failing? You are too afraid to fail, and what others might say, so you never even begin on that healthy journey or start that new business that will provide your family with the money and time freedom you have always dreamed of. Or maybe it's the mountain of debt that has just become overwhelming, and you are choosing not to focus on it because you see no way out. There are many mountains, my friends, that will try to stand in your way. Debt, Divorce, Disease, Discouragement, Addiction, and so on. These are all things that are real-life scenarios that we face every day.

However, the good news is that you don't have to let this be your reality. See, I believe that once we take whatever has been holding us back, the mountain in our life, and we decide that we will no longer let that keep us from living the life we desire, it is a game changer. Now we must back that decision with action. Jesus says, "Cast it into the sea! Have you ever lost anything at sea? It makes me think of the movie Titanic, where at the end of the movie, Rose throws the necklace out into the sea. It is now gone. When you lose something out at sea, and it sinks, it is gone. Jesus says, "Throw it into the sea. That mountain you have been dealing with, the addiction you are deciding to give up once and for all, that spouse that you are committing to love and take divorce off the table, that disease that you are no longer going to allow to run your life because somebody said you will always have it and there's no cure.

JESUS IS THE CURE

Trust me, there is a cure, and His name is Jesus. I have seen this in my own life with myself and my wife first-hand. Whatever it is, Jesus says that we must not doubt and believe that what we say will happen. Then it will be done for you. See, too many times, we say we want something, ask God for it, and then later that day, we begin to doubt it's possible. Our own doubt kills the seed before it even has a chance to take root and start growing. When I made the decision to quit smoking marijuana on March 15, 2010, I was done. I had literally thrown all our stuff away, cast it into the sea of our toilet, and flushed it away. I declared with my words that this was the last time I would ever smoke marijuana again, and there wasn't one doubt that I was ever going back. I had a decided heart at that time. When my wife and I decided to burn the boats and create a beautiful marriage instead of living in chaos all the time, we had to take the word "divorce" off the table and cast it into the sea. That was no longer an option. What was an option was that each of us would focus on the person in the mirror, praying for each other daily, serving each other, getting professional help from a marriage coach, and trusting in God that the union he brought together was meant to stay together. Now 17 years later, I am married to my best friend, and we have a beautiful marriage. To think at one point we didn't even like each other, let alone love each other in our marriage, is just a testament to what God can do when we put our faith and trust in Him and take action on His teachings.

So I will end with verse 24 as it is an example of how visualization works, in my opinion. **Jesus says, "Therefore I tell you, whatever you ask for in prayer, believe that you have received it, and it will be yours!"** Now let's think about this for a second. Are you seeing what I am seeing? He literally just said, "Whatever you ask for in prayer, which to me means whatever, anything, just like ALL means ALL, which you will see all throughout scripture. Believe that you have received it, and it will be yours! Now, if he is telling us to believe that we have received it, whatever it is for you, what does that mean? I believe that means that whatever "IT" is that you want, a more loving marriage, more money, a healthier body, more peace, breaking free from an addiction and living a life filled with more fulfillment, a life filled with abundance, freedom, and victory in every area my friends! See IT as yours. He is saying that we have to believe first before we can ever receive. Now that we believe, we will generally begin and then become friends! If you believe that you have received something, it is yours. You don't have to keep hoping for it. It is already yours! His peace is already yours! You've already got the ability to break free from that addiction. The money that you desire is already yours. The marriage that you desire, you can actually create in your mind first, and because you start to focus on what you want versus what you don't want, things begin to change in the direction you desire. Man, this stuff is powerful!

YOU HAVE THE POWER TO CREATE!

See, **all things are created twice, friends. First, they are created in the mind and then in reality.** Anything that you see today, from a car driving on the road to a massive building to the house you live in, the couch you sit on, the TV you watch, etc., was first a thought that became an imagination in someone's mind. See, we have the ability to do the same thing, and God's word backs it up. We can pray to him for anything. We can believe in it, and I believe we can expect it to happen. Now, like the scripture says, we can't go around doubting all day long. No, we've got to give thanks to God in advance. Every day, thank him for giving you the strength to overcome the temptations that come your way. Every day, he gives you the ability and creativity to build successful businesses. Every day, thank him for that spouse that challenges you to step up and raise your standards as the leader of your house. That was a big one for me because early in our marriage, Rachel just wanted me to step up and quit acting like a kid. It was time for me to choose my family over hanging out with the guys at the bar, after softball league, or on a work day.

So as I wrap up the Power of Visualization, friends, trust me when I say this can be one of the most powerful things that you can do on a daily basis to create the right mindset each day and accelerate you in creating the Champion Life that you desire to live and that God desires for you and me. It is 100% worth building in 5-10 minutes a day in your Hour of Power to do it consistently each day.

DEVELOPING AN ATTITUDE OF GRATITUDE

Gratitude: The last thing that I like to do is go over 2-3 things that I am grateful for that day and why. **Gratitude is the antidote to all negativity.** If you are ever feeling off, frustrated, bitter, fearful, etc., The quickest way out of these negative feelings is to ask yourself this question. **What am I grateful for?** Then if you really want to intensify the feeling of gratitude, ask yourself: Why are you grateful for what you said? By the way, it doesn't have to be something big to be grateful for. Right now, you could probably find ten things that you are grateful for that you could easily begin to start focusing on each day, or anytime you are feeling stuck, in a negative mindset, etc. Actually, let's do this! Let's go ahead and write down three things right now. Remember, this book is all about action! I will even give you some potential things, but I want you to choose what is true for you. Here are just a few of mine. Feel free to steal 1 or 2 of them, but I really want you to think about what is good in your life.

Here is what I am grateful for at this exact moment I am writing this book on this Friday morning, October 29, 2021, at 6:19 AM! I am grateful for:

- My Personal Relationship with Jesus and the fact that He Loves Me Just the Way I Am!
- I am grateful for my Health and that I have a strong healthy body that allows me to do the things I love to do everyday!
- I am grateful for my wife, who loves Jesus. She takes great care of herself, and she is obedient to the call on her life.
- I am grateful for my children and how healthy they are, their awesome personalities, and the gifts God has given each of them.
- I am grateful for the businesses I have been given to produce wealth for my family while getting to serve so many people, doing what I love each day.
- I am grateful that every morning I get to wake up in a warm bed, under a roof, and get to take a shower with warm water if I choose.
- I am grateful that I have a car that I get to drive to my office daily vs. having to walk or ride a bike, which I have had to do at one point in my life.
- I am grateful to the incredible mentors and coaches who have poured into my life, helping me to develop a champion mindset that has opened up a whole new world to me.
- I am grateful for the amazing trips that our family has been able to go on over the years to places like Rome, Paris, the Caribbean, and the Cruise with my momma!

- I am grateful for our dogs, who greet me every day when I walk in the door with love and excitement like they haven't seen me in a year.
- I am grateful for the fridge stocked with food, clean water from our reverse osmosis system, and even a garage fridge filled with drinks.
- I am grateful for this home office I am sitting in that allows me to work from home many times and has a nice desk and a comfortable chair.
- I am grateful for my church, Victory Church, and my pastor, Andy, who has become a great friend, workout partner, and person to give and receive encouragement.
- I am grateful to my little bro, TJ, with whom I get to spend my days building businesses, playing golf, having fun, visioning ideas, and simply having fun!
- I am grateful for the men I get to serve each day with Champion Builders, my coaching program, and for seeing them break through to new levels.

Okay, I think I just listed 15 in like 5 minutes! I could keep going, but this is about you, not me. I just want to share with you that if you learn to ask this question, "What am I grateful for and why?" It can change your life! So now it's your turn. Go ahead and take a second to write down a few things you are grateful for an why!

Gratitude List
WRITE THE TOP 3 THINGS YOU ARE GRATEFUL FOR, AND WHY

1. _____
BECAUSE:
1. _____
2. _____
3. _____

2. _____
BECAUSE:
1. _____
2. _____
3. _____

3. _____
BECAUSE:
1. _____
2. _____
3. _____

**Meditate and Visualize for 10 minutes, 3 times this week.
Journal how you feel after.**

Sunday ☐   Wednesday ☐
Monday ☐   Thursday ☐
Tuesday ☐   Friday ☐
                Saturday ☐

CHAMPION BUILDERS ACADEMY
LIFE, LEADERSHIP, & BUSINESS COACHING

Awesome. Now think about those things just for a second. We take many things that are so good in our lives for granted. Most of the world lives on $2 a day, doesn't have access to clean water to drink, and in many countries, they can't even openly share that they love Jesus. This is the truth, my friend. So those are just three more things that we can be grateful for. So can I encourage you to take 2 minutes and think about three things you are grateful for and Why as you go through your morning routine each morning? It will be life changing!

CHAPTER 4

CREATING YOUR NEW IDENTITY

THE POWER OF I AM & IDENTITY

6:05 AM—I AM STATEMENTS

Alright, friends, buckle up on this section because this might just be the most powerful part of your Hour of Power each day. **The Power of I AM STATEMENTS can absolutely change your life because I believe that we think, feel, and act each day based upon who we think we are.** Here is what I mean. We all have an identity. It is basically what we believe to be true about ourselves. This identity governs pretty much everything you do in your life, whether you realize it or not. It is made up of your thoughts, beliefs, life experiences, etc. It is pretty much the computer software that runs your life. This is why when we go to change something in our life, it feels very uncomfortable, and we tend to not even want to try, or if we do, we quit after a short period of time, because even though on a conscious level we say we want whatever it is, our subconscious overrides it.

THE LAW OF THE THERMOSTAT

Let me give you a couple of examples of what I mean when I say, "your subconscious overrides it." See, your identity governs your life much like the thermostat in your home governs the temperature. When your home is set at 70 degrees, for instance, and it gets cold outside, the thermostat will kick on the heat to automatically regulate the room temperature back up to 70. The same is true if it gets too hot. It will kick on the AC to cool down the house and get it back to 70. The key point that I want to make here and then share how this applies to your life is the "70-degree rule." Why does the temperature always go back to 70 degrees? The reason is that; that is the temperature you have programmed your thermostat to stay at. Therefore, it does its job, and it stays right there no matter what the outside temperature is.

See, every area of our life has a set point, just like your thermostat at home. It is what I like to refer to as our comfort zone. We are comfortable right where we are. By the way, this rule applies to any area of your life. Your body, your finances, your marriage, and so on. Let's use your body as an example, as I have seen this happen first hand over the years while working with thousands of people on their health and fitness, owning gyms, and being in the fitness business. Most people have a set point physically as to where they feel comfortable. A certain weight, body fat, look, etc. If you begin to put on some weight and not feel so good about yourself, you will naturally say, "Whoa, I need to start working out again and eat a little bit cleaner." Naturally, you drop some weight, start feeling a little better, and get back to that set point. Now you keep going, keep pushing, and actually go to the next level, and you're feeling amazing about yourself. However, a couple of months go by, and you find yourself slacking off, missing a couple of workouts, having a few more desserts, and before you know it, you are back to your set point, ideal weight, etc. You keep up with those habits, and a few months from there, you have put back the same 10 or 20 you lost, and you're back starting the process all over again. "What happened," you might ask yourself. What happened is that you never changed your set point. Don't worry. I will show you how to change your setpoint here in a second, so you won't have to deal with this again!

How about your finances? Have you ever been in a situation where you were like, "I need to make more money, focus on my budget, pay off some debt," and you did it? You may have increased how much you earn over a month or two by taking some more action, talking to a few more customers, etc. You were heating up, really crushing it in your business or profession. You knocked out the debt, put some money in your savings, and are riding high! Then, six months later, you find out that you somehow wiped out your savings. You're no longer hustling the way you were, and fast forward six months, and you're back in debt. Once again, you're asking yourself, "What happened?" So what do you do? You begin the process over, heating back up to get back to your comfort zone.

The last example I will give you is in your marriage. I have played this game many times over the years. Rachel and I are not doing so well, and I realize I am focusing way too much on business and outside interests and not on her. So naturally, that affects the relationship. It cools things off just right. The passion and intimacy aren't as hot, especially in the bedroom, guys. The reason why is that our wives aren't feeling loved. <u>We, as men, are like microwaves when it comes to sex. We can be ready in a minute. However, our wives are like crock pots. They need to be turned on early in the day, with some love, attention, a listening ear, and a compliment</u>. So when this doesn't happen, guess what? Yep, you guessed it; we're not getting the good loving that night! We have all been there. So, back to my point. We start doing things to heat up our marriage again; we buy our wife a gift, clean the house, and take her on some dates. One of the biggest things I recommend is praying with our wives and for them. I will talk about that more later in the book. Before you know it, our marriage is flying high, and we are loving life. Things have heated up, and we love being married again. Then it happens; we stop doing what we were doing to heat things up. The marriage cools back down to our set point, and then eventually, it cools off so much that we have to turn back up the heat again to get back to normal. For most people, this is a yearly thing, by the way. In people's fitness and health, it's normally every January. I hope you are seeing a pattern here and maybe how this has played out in your own life at times. So the question is: how do we stop this madness from happening? I'm glad you asked!

CREATE A NEW SETPOINT

It's time to create a new you! A New Identity! A new set point, if you will, in your health, marriage, finances, etc. The quickest way I have learned to get to the next level in my life is by doing three things.

The first is that who you hang out with matters. If I am 70 degrees in my health and fitness, I need to begin to hang out with people that have their fitness at 100 degrees. I call this the "Power of Association." I have a friend named Valerie. She is a former IFBB pro figure champion and played Siren on the TV show American Gladiators. She is the type of person that truly values her health and wellness, stays in good shape year-round, and takes great care of her body. Every time I am around her, I feel as though I need to level up my fitness because of her commitment to fitness. You want somebody like Valerie in your life who inspires you to go to the next level. If your workout partner is the type of person that when you call and say, "hey, I'm not going to go to the gym today, and they know you have some big goals, and they say, okay, no biggie, you might want to find a new workout partner with more commitment.

There is a powerful teaching that I heard many years ago that made me really think and make some changes in my life. It says **five years from now, you will be the average of the five people you hang out with the most.** If you hang out with five broke people, there is a good chance you will be broke too. If you hang out with five alcoholics, there is a good chance you will be drinking every day right along with them. If you hang out with five divorced men who cheated on their wives, you will have a good chance of ending up in the same boat. The opposite is true, though. If you hang out with five people who go to the gym every day, eat clean, and take care of their bodies daily, you will be fit and in shape. This is such a powerful truth, my friend!

I used to get into so much trouble in our marriage because when Rachel and I would get into a fight, I would meet up with a friend at the bar and talk about my problems; as you can imagine, that only led to more problems. Then I changed one thing. I started to change who I met and where I met, and things began to change. Instead of meeting a friend with a messed-up relationship himself in a bar, I started meeting men from my church with great marriages over a cup of coffee to get wisdom. As you can imagine, these Men, I would consider to be at 100 degrees in their marriage. So naturally, because I was hanging around them more often, my set point in my marriage began to rise. I was no longer at 70 but at 85 just from being around them.

I will give you one last example. This has happened in my business life. As I started to hang out with people who were wealthy financially, I began to heat up. I began to make more money. I was also giving more to my church because I noticed that all the men I was hanging out with had a deep belief in generosity. They had an abundant mindset when it came to money. I am excited to share more on this subject later in this book. I hope you are picking up what I am throwing down here. What I am saying is, chances are you will have to weed out some people in your life and get some new people to hang out with if you want to heat up in your life, marriage, business, health, etc. I will add one more thing that I believe is very important and has truly impacted me over the last ten years. These three words "Raise Your Standards" have been a great focus for me in so many ways, helping me to heat up my life and never go back to the old Curt I used to be. I am excited to share this concept with you because I know If you too ask yourself how you can, each day, it will be a game changer. So let me show you how!

RAISE YOUR STANDARDS

The second thing after you change who you're hanging out with is to raise your standards. It really begins with raising your standards! **If we want to change our lives, we have to raise our standards.** As we begin to raise our standards of what we are willing to accept as our normal, as our comfort zone, things begin to change. See, as I gave you, examples related to fitness, marriage, and money. It really applies to anything in your life. So, just like the way your house thermostat works, if you wanted your home to stay at 80 degrees no matter the outside conditions, you would need to first, set a new set point. Then the system knows what to do. So now, let's begin to talk about how you can set new set points in your life, so you can go to the next level and create what I like to refer to as The Champion Life. A life filled with abundance, freedom, and victory where you are winning in your faith, fitness, family, finances, and having fun! It all starts by raising your standards and creating a new identity. Get a new vision for your life, the things you want, and who you are. See, if you are going to be able to raise your standards, you are going to first need to upgrade your software, aka your mindset and belief systems, before you can expect different results. There is a reason why we are not using Windows 3 on our computers anymore or IOS 7 on our iPhones. Things have advanced and gotten better, and so should we. So let's talk about how we upgrade. It really starts with creating that new identity, and I am going to show you three ways to do that right now!

THE POWER OF I AM STATEMENTS

I know that we have already talked a lot about mindset. The reason why is that this is such a crucial part of creating a Champion Life. Before you can ever have a Champion Life, you will have to first create a Champion Mindset. Remember what I said earlier? All things are created twice. First in the mind and then in reality. Too many people try to accomplish goals, and when they fail, they have no idea why. Most of the time, it was because their mindset was off. It's like somebody in a hurry to get to a meeting for work, driving 90 on the highway going as fast as they can to get there, only to realize 15 minutes into the drive that they got on the wrong freeway and they're going North instead of South. I'm sure we've all done that, and it stinks. It is frustrating! So what do we do? We sometimes need to slow down so we can speed up. Let's make sure that we are going in the right direction. Once we know we are going in the right direction, we have a vision, goals, and the right mindset, we can take massive action on those goals, putting the pedal to the metal and going as fast as we can!

So as I get into the power of **I AM STATEMENTS,** I want you to think about these as a seed that you are planting and nurturing every day. It is a seed because your mind is like a garden. That is a great way to view your mind. Let me explain. There are really three stages to a garden, much like a mindset.

STAGE 1 - PREPARATION

The first thing that we have to do to create a beautiful garden is to go through and tear out all the weeds. Clean up all the stuff that the wind has blown in etc. The most important thing is that we have to dig out any roots that are under the soil because if we don't, they will continue to grow weeds, and who knows what around the new seeds we have planted. This is so critical. If we don't do this work, we will not have a beautiful garden. Well, just like the garden, we have to do this work in our own minds. **What are the weeds, and most importantly, the roots in your mind, that you need to get rid of?** What limiting beliefs have you chosen to believe about yourself? What things from your past do you need to let go of? What fear of the future do you keep thinking about that stops you from taking the action you need? You have to let go of these, my friends, to live the Champion Life that God has for you. That is why one of the things I define as living the Champion Life is FREEDOM!

✈ <u>Too many people are living in prison cells in their minds, but the door is open, and you can walk out at any time.</u>

The enemy has convinced us, though, that we can't. We have conditioned ourselves to focus on the wrong things, on lies, and now we aren't able to break free. It's like a baby circus elephant when they are born. The first thing the trainer does is attach them to a stake in the ground when they aren't strong enough to break free from it. The baby elephant tries and tries to break free, and eventually, it can't because, at that point in its life, it is too small and not powerful enough to, so it gives up. It literally gives up forever. Then the Elephant becomes this massive 10,000-pound creature that could literally rip a massive tree out of the ground, but yet because it has been conditioned, it can't even rip a tiny stake that they have attached it to. That still blows my mind when I think about up concept and how true it is. We have all seen this firsthand at a circus.

So what I am here to tell you today is the truth. The truth is we have the power, my friends; we just have to use it! I understand that things have happened to you. I understand there have been some failures, some wrong-doings, and some dysfunction. I am a walking example of a person who grew up in a dysfunctional family. I have already shared that part of my journey. However, for you, you must identify these lies that the enemy has been feeding you, the things from your past that are stopping you from moving forward, and set yourself free! Nobody is going to do it for you or me. We have to do the work and take care of our own garden. So can I encourage you before we move on to identify 1 or 2 things that need to be uprooted in your life before we begin to create the seed and start the planting process? If you don't, you won't be able to have the beautiful garden that is possible.

I will give you a couple of mine, and then I would recommend you put down two or three. Here are three of my biggest lies that I needed to uproot.

1. I had to get rid of all my daddy issues and being upset with him because he wasn't there for me growing up. I had a lot of hatred toward him because of how he treated my mom and all his broken promises. So that root of bitterness, unforgiveness, anger, etc. was removed, which set me free to just love him, give him grace, pray for him, and most importantly, just focus on what I needed to do to not make the same mistakes and give my kids the Dad that I always desired.

2. The second root I needed to give up was that I wasn't good enough. I wasn't smart enough to succeed in life and business. I didn't graduate high school or go to college. I experienced being broken and bankrupt. All

this stuff for years would be what my mind focused on. Yes, all of the above is true, but those were just events in my life. That didn't have to define me. So I had to rip that stuff out of my mind and replace it with the truth. I am more than enough. I can do all things through Christ who strengthens me.

3. The last one, which I already told you about, was getting rid of the dependency on drugs. That was a lie that I had chosen to believe for too long. It was rooted in my mindset and belief system that I was better off smoking weed every day. It calmed me down, helped me sleep, made me more creative, etc. The truth was that it made me lazy, eat a bunch of food at night, and not care about stuff in my life that I really needed to change. It was a band-aid for my emotions. When I ripped that out of my life, in less than one year, I had doubled my income, and my mindset had never been clearer.

So now it's your turn, my friend. What is it that you need to let go of? What thing from your past do you want to have uprooted? What meaning do you need to give to the past hurt that harmed you, a failed relationship or business, or even a new venture that you would like to embark upon? Take a second to clean out some weeds, uproot these past hurts or even future fears, and let's get started on planting some powerful I AM STATEMENTS that will become the seed for a new harvest that, trust me, you are going to like. So take a second to write down a few below, and then let's get to planting some seeds!

LET IT GO

What are three things that you are letting go of today, uprooting from your life and mindset, that has been holding you back from living the Champion Life God has created for you?

1.
2.
3.

Great job, my friend! This isn't an easy process, but it is very necessary for renewing your mind and living a Champion Life. Okay, now let's start to plant what you want in your life.

STAGE 2 - PLANTING

Now that we have done the work and prepared our garden, it's time to start putting in the seed. The seed, if you remember, is your I AM STATEMENTS and YOUR GOALS! These are the things that you will begin to FOCUS on every day, nurture with daily repetition and action, and just like in a garden if we do it right over time, it is pretty much a lock that we will begin to see the things we planted begin to grow! So now, what we want to do is begin to think about what we want in our life. The way I like to write my "I am" statements is in the form of what I want in my life. I write them in the present tense as well. As you remember, earlier in this book, I referenced Jesus in Mark 11:24 telling the disciples. **"Therefore, I tell you, whatever you ask for in prayer, believe that you have received it, and it will be yours."** He didn't say, "Hope that it will happen; maybe you will get it someday." **He said, "Believe that you have received it**, not that you are going to receive it." See, I believe that we need to speak about what we want in a way that we already have it. It is ours. We are that person now, and because we choose to focus on it that way, it naturally tends to happen. I have seen this work firsthand in my life over and over. When creating a new identity, which begins with a new mindset, it first starts with the way you see yourself. What is your character? Jesus did this in the gospels. There are many times recorded where He said, "I am statements." I will give you a couple of examples.

> 1. "I Am the Bread of Life" (John 6). 2. "I Am the Light of the World" (John 8). 3. "I Am the Gate of the Sheepfold" (John 10). 4. "I Am the Good Shepherd" (John 10). 5. "I Am the Resurrection and the Life" (John 11). 6. "I Am the Way, Truth, and Life" (John 14). 7. I Am the True Vine: Jesus is the source of eternal life for us who are dead and useless branches apart from him (John 15).

So, as you begin to think about who you truly desire to be and what you desire to do with your life, I would encourage you to develop your I am statements in a way that aligns with these. These will be the seeds that you will plant in your mind; nurture them daily during your morning hour of power, focus on them every day, and watch yourself grow into the Champion God created you to be. As I read my, "I am" statements every morning and sometimes throughout the day, I like to see myself living out these statements. This is me. This is my life. Even though maybe some of the things I am saying aren't my reality just yet, that's okay. This is the direction that I want my life to go. I am filling my mind with what I want to produce more of in my life. I no longer desire the old me; being broke financially, having no peace, fighting all the time in my marriage, being filled with fear, worry, and doubt, having no purpose, etc. That is old. I am no longer that person, and that is not my life. Those have been ripped out, uprooted, and now new seeds are being prepared for harvest.

This concept, friends, is why I love these two powerful verses that are foundational for my life. 2 Corinthians 5:17 "We are new creations in Christ Jesus. The old is gone, the new is here!" The other is Romans 12:2 "Be transformed by the renewing of your mind." When we truly understand the power of this, it is life-changing.

I hope this gets you excited, my friend! So what do you say we start creating some new powerful I am statements that will lead your life to the next level? I am going to share with you the exact "I am" statements that I have in my journal right now. As you know, I am an open book. I have nothing to hide, and I have one reason for sharing this with you. That it will give you some ideas, maybe inspire you, and that you will know what is most important to me in my life. As you read through mine, I want you to think: Do any of these align with some of the things that you want to be, do, or have in your life? If they do, great, feel free to steal them, use them for yourself, but attach whatever meaning you want to them. Every one of my I am statements has a deeper meaning to it, and I will explain a couple in detail here in a second that I believe will make this process even better for you. So here are mine as of right now, Oct 30, 2021!

I AM Curt Tucker! I AM a Champion Leader and Champion Builder who is Courageous, Confident, Consistent, and Committed work with Excellence until the Completion of God's Purpose and Mission for my life! Yes, you are!

I AM A Champion For Christ!
I AM A Loving & Encouraging Husband, Father, and Leader!

I AM Healthy, Wealthy, and Wise!
I AM A Man who gives Excellence In All I do!
I AM A Smart and Savvy Businessman and Investor, Who is a Multimillionaire, A Great Steward of God's Wealth, and A Generous Giver.
I Can Learn and Master Any Skill!
I Live Everyday Like It's An Adventure!
I AM Filled with God's Love and Grace and Guided by His Holy Spirit!
I AM Earning $100,000 a month or more by Jan 31, 2022!
I AM the number one giver in our church!
I AM the Owner of a Beautiful Beach Front property by June 1, 2022!
I AM the Owner/Investor of a $2 Million Dollar or more Apartment Complex!
I AM a Highly Sought after Speaker, Preacher, Coach, and Podcast Host!
I AM a Best-Selling Author!

Alright, now you know everything about me! Some people say you shouldn't tell people your goals because all they will do is tell you every reason why you can't accomplish them. I agree with this 100%. However, I know if you have chosen to buy this book and read it this far, you are not a person looking to judge me, but hopefully, learn, and that is the purpose of this book. To inspire you to create your own Champion Life, whatever that looks like for you!

So, as you can see, I have written these statements out in a way that clearly describes what I want to be more of in my life, what I want to do more of in my life, and even what I want to have more of in my life. Of course, I want to be a loving and encouraging husband and father. I will tell you that I haven't always been that, but now I am! I am healthy, wealthy, and wise! How can I confidently say that? I can because every day I do this Hour of Power every day, workout, eat well, seek wisdom, and all the other things we are talking about in this book. Once again, this wasn't always me. I had to make some serious changes. One of my favorites is I am Filled with God's Love and Grace and Guided by His Holy Spirit. These I am statements bring me so much joy, peace, and freedom. The truth is that every day I have a God that loves me no matter what, that His grace is everlasting no matter how messed up I am or how many mistakes I make. The fact that I have the choice to be led by His Spirit is powerful. I don't want to operate in my flesh alone. When I do that, I tend to mess things up. **However, when the power of the Holy Spirit guides me, all things are possible in my life!**

What about the money? I will discuss this subject later in the book, but yes, I want to earn more money. Having more money allows me to give more to my family, give more to my church, and live the lifestyle I desire. This is part of being abundant!

Okay, now it's time for you to create some of your own, my friend! I want to encourage you to really think about what you want to be more of in your life, what you want to do, and even things you would like to have. Write them in the form of an "I am" statement below. I have given you some spots to write here in this book, and then what I would really encourage you to do is write them in your journal so that you can look at them every day. I actually just typed mine up on a Google doc, printed them off, and taped them to the front page of my journal. That is a hack that took me years to figure out!

Alright, Champion, what do you desire in your life? Go ahead and write some down!

My I am statements!

1.
2.
3
4.
5.

Great job, Champion! Like I said before, feel free to write out even more and put them in your journal that you will be using for your morning devotion, goals, etc. This way, you will have everything in one place. Read them aloud each morning, while you're on the treadmill, on your lunch break, or even right before you go to bed. Trust me when I say you will feel inspired every time you do it, especially if you truly believe in your heart that this is you and that it's possible. Which it is, I am living proof, and most importantly, Jesus says so. Mark 9:23 says, "All things are possible to those who believe!"

AS A MAN THINKS, SO SHALL HE BECOME

STAGE 3 - REAP THE HARVEST

Alright, are you ready to hear some exciting stuff? So here is the deal! When you consistently begin to do what I have outlined above, something magical happens. You begin to reap the harvest of what you want more of in your life. I sometimes don't even know how to explain it; other than that, it just happens. We just tend to get more of what we focus on in life. This goes for the good or the bad. I remember when all I used to focus on was how broke I was. It would consume me, day in and day out. Then, as I learned this principle and I began to focus on all the good in my life, I began to change my money mindset, which we will talk about later, and boom, things began to change! If you truly understand the farming process, or in this case, if we have been talking about a garden, things just tend to happen. It is by God's design. When you prepare the soil correctly, you plant something and continue to nurture it with what it needs to grow. Eventually, that seed will grow into whatever seed you planted. It is what it is. We don't question it when we are planting vegetables. So why do we question this process when it comes to what we want in life? We let doubt get in the way. We let past failures and experiences get in the way. I don't care what seeds you have planted in the past; they don't have anything to do with the future. Whatever you plant and nurture over time will grow! So can I encourage you today to plant more Abundance, Gratitude, Love, etc. Plant the things that you want more of in your life, focus on them daily during your Hour of Power and throughout your day, and watch a beautiful life grow right in front of you!

CHAPTER 5

BEING FIT FOR YOUR MISSION

EXERCISE IS THE BEST DRUG, DRINK, OR PROZAC YOU CAN EVER TAKE!

As I think about the things that are most important in creating a Champion Life, being strong and fit are very high on the list. That is why a big part of my morning routine, a daily ritual, is some form of exercise. **Exercise, in my opinion, is the best drug, drink, or Prozac you can ever take.** There are so many scientific things that are happening in your body when you are exercising. Your body releases all kinds of endorphins that make you feel good, and who doesn't want to feel good? Well, that can be debatable. What do I mean by that? Great question. I believe that too many people have become so used to feeling like crap that this is their common state of being. No energy, negative mindset, glass half empty attitude, and because that is their program, they live that over and over. That is why addictions are a thing. We then go to negative comfort to help us cope with this addiction. It could be sugar, alcohol, hard drugs, or even certain pharmaceutical drugs. I'm just saying, have you tried things like exercising every day first, putting great nutrition in your body, and practicing a healthy morning routine like I have been talking about in the first part of this book?

We know that the body follows the mind. I love the saying, **"Where the mind goes, the man follows."** Often, when I'm speaking with somebody who has an addiction to cigarettes or marijuana or is on some type of depression or anxiety medication, the first thing I ask them is, "Do you exercise?" and 99% of the time, the answer is no. This actually hurts my heart, as I am such a big supporter of working out daily, and I know what they don't know, which is that they don't have to live the way they're living. They don't have to be dependent on these drugs. I believe in this wholeheartedly, and I have seen this firsthand absolutely transform people's lives over the years, owning gyms and helping people with their fitness and nutrition. I have helped people kick addictions to certain drugs, alcohol, and cigarettes many times. One of the first things that I get them to do is put down the addiction and pick up a new addiction, a healthy addiction like working out every day. It's funny how when you think you need a cigarette, and instead of smoking a cigarette, you get down and bust out 10 or 20 pushups, you don't feel like smoking for that time period. Your lungs are saying, "Please don't fill me with that garbage; just let me get some fresh air!" This is what we call a "pattern interrupt," by the way

See, for years, when you're used to doing something over and over again, it is just natural that you do it subconsciously. Now, if all of sudden you feel that desire to smoke, have that drink, eat the sweet, you instead run down the street and back, go to the gym, bust out some pushups, or anything active, you begin to create those new neural pathways in your brain, while also giving your body all kinds of healing chemicals. Your body begins to feel better every single day. You have more energy, the weight begins to come off, and you feel great both mentally and physically. So if we know that exercise is so good for us, and most of us do, then why don't we do it? I believe it is because, just like anything else, we haven't made it important enough. We haven't created meaning around exercise and taking care of our health that says this is a must. Some people do after they have had something life-altering happen to them, like cancer, a heart attack, or being diagnosed with diabetes. I see this happen all the time in the fitness business. The thing is, why wait until you have all these health issues to make your health a priority?

MAKE EXERCISE FUN

So what I want to do in this section of the book is make it really easy for you to take back control of your health and encourage you to focus on making exercise a part of your everyday lifestyle. One of the big keys is to make it fun! When you have more energy and feel better, you will be better at everything you do. It is just the facts. So I am going to encourage you to give yourself 30 minutes a day to do some type of exercise. It could be running, lifting weights, yoga, cycling, rebounding, or whatever. Just get moving. Now I am a huge fan of lifting weights for the simple fact that you need muscle. As we get older and we lose muscle, simple daily tasks become harder to do. There are too many people in nursing homes at a relatively young age because they can't do basic things like take a shower, use the bathroom, cook, and so on by themselves. You may not be in that boat, but if you are a mid-40s wife and mom who has been trying to lose weight for years by doing cardio and counting calories. Trust me when I say you need to lift some weights! When you build muscles, you build your metabolism! If you don't know what to do, make an investment in yourself and hire a trainer. Notice I didn't say just join a gym. No, I said to hire a trainer, a professional, somebody who knows what they're doing and can help you.

Lastly, I think about us guys. It is undeniable that **when you are fit and strong, you are more confident**! It doesn't take very long to develop some great muscles if you actually train them and then feed them the right nutrition to help them recover, repair, and ultimately grow. So here is what I am going to do. I am going to give you a couple of great resources to start you off in this book, and then you have to take it from there. You have to make exercising daily a priority, set aside time daily, and most importantly, show up! This is another reason why I am such a big fan of hiring a coach or joining a training program because you will get the accountability that most people lack. In my gyms, it is so cool to see our clients show up and actually have fun working out together! It is a game changer when you know you have a coach waiting for you and a group of people to work out with. That or a great workout partner is the next best thing, but make sure that your workout partner is committed. Meaning they actually show up and don't make excuses, like "Hey, let's just work out tomorrow" kinda attitude. That is not the type of workout partner you want to have as a friend. You want somebody as committed as you, or better yet, even more, committed!

TO WIN, YOU MUST BEGIN

Okay, so we have talked about the importance of exercise and all the benefits, and we know that we need to do it. So now what? Well, it really boils down to just going and taking action. I love to say, **"To Win, you must Begin!"** Nothing happens without some type of action. There is a joke that says five frogs were sitting on a lily pad when one decided to jump. How many frogs are now left on the lily pad? Most people will say four. Simple math, right? Five minus one equals four. Well, actually, the answer is still five. How is that? Well, nobody said that the frog actually jumped off. What was said was that "he decided." A decision must be backed with action by friends. So we must make the decision and then take action!

I am going to just share with you what I do on a daily basis from an exercise standpoint. I'm not perfect, but it works for me and my busy schedule. I have a busy life: married, with four kids, running three businesses, and a lot going on. I don't have hours to spend in the gym every day, so I'm looking to commit just 30 minutes a day to exercise. While exercising, I often listen to something positive in an area I want to grow in, like my marriage, mindset, business, etc. I call this "NET" time, meaning "No Extra Time." It is a hack where you can maximize your time by doing two things at once. So I am a huge believer in continually learning and getting better every day. **If you're not growing daily, you're dying gradually.** So as I do my cardio on the treadmill three times a week for 30 minutes, and then for 5-10 minutes after my lifting days, three days a week, I will listen to a podcast, YouTube video, or audiobook. I will also use this time to read through my I am statements and goals in my journal or even look at my vision board if I'm at my house. I have a gym in my basement, and I leave my vision board hanging up on the wall right in front of my treadmill, so anytime I want to look at it, I just jump on it and start walking! See, this stuff isn't rocket science like some people make it out to be.

So, as I said above, I keep it really simple. I generally do some type of strength training Mon-Wed-Fri with weights for 20-30 minutes, followed by 10 minutes of HIIT cardio, which stands for High-Intensity Interval Training, and then stretch. On Tues-Thurs-Sat, I usually just do 20-30 minutes of HIIT cardio with a couple of core and ab exercises. This type of workout split works very well for me with my schedule and is easy to follow.

If you are willing to give yourself 30 minutes a day, preferably in the morning, you will absolutely be able to transform your physical body within a matter of a month or two. Of course, you have to keep going if you want to maintain it, and that is why I believe in 30 minutes a day, not 2 hours a day. That is why all my group workouts at my gyms for our clients are designed for around 30 minutes. Anything worth doing is worth doing consistently, especially if it makes you feel amazing! You might not always feel amazing during the workout, but you do afterward.

I can guarantee you that if you do it for a month, you will see great results and how easy it is to fit into your day. So as I say, this book is all about action. So go ahead and write down your goals for the next 30 or even 90 days in your fitness, and get going! Keep it simple, friend! Set 1 or 2 goals, and just give yourself 30 minutes a day, and watch what happens! You will feel absolutely amazing! Also, can I encourage you to take a before pic? Trust me when I say you might not like the before, but you will love the after. Then you will be able to see how far you have come and the transformation, and that will give you confidence in the next goal you set. If 90 days is too much to focus on, then start with 30 days. As I have said multiple times, **the best investment you can make is in yourself.** So give yourself the gift of exercise and invest these 30 minutes daily in yourself.

Write out your 90 Day physical goals:
Ex: weight, body fat, 5k, etc.
_____
_____
_____

Write out a workout program that you are committed to doing for the next 30 days:
_____
_____
_____

Complete your first HIIT Cardio & Weight Training workout for upper & lower body:

	Sun	Mon	Tues	Wed	Thurs	Fri	Sat
HIIT							
weights: upper body							
weights: lower body							

Take Before Picture

CHAMPION BUILDERS ACADEMY
LIFE, LEADERSHIP, & BUSINESS COACHING

THE MORNING MATTERS

Many people ask me why I am such a huge fan of the morning workout versus at lunch or even in the evening after work. I have a few major reasons why, but first, let me say this. Just like investing in real estate, yourself, or anything else, the best time is NOW. The best time is to just get in the game. Start doing something! So the point is, anytime is a great time to work out each day!

For me, there are three major reasons why I choose the morning, and I would encourage you to do the same. Here they are.

1. TIMING: The reality is that we are all busy. That word "busy," by the way, is the number one excuse I hear from most people when they say they don't exercise. They say I don't have time. I am just too busy. When somebody tells me that, I don't judge them; I just challenge them to realign their priorities. See, **we all have 24 hours in a day. It really is the number one equalizer that we all have in this life.** All of us don't have the same background, skin color, or education level, but we do have the same 86,400 seconds each day to decide how we want to spend it. Like I said earlier, we can waste it or invest it. It is totally up to us. Some people have plenty of time to watch hours of Netflix each week or scroll through Facebook, but they don't have time to work out for 30 minutes. This is just a waste of time.

Now, what about the legitimate reasons that we could miss, like I have work deadlines, kids' sports, and I serve at church? I have heard all these as well, and yes, they are valid, but not a reason to stop you from giving your body what it needs each day. I choose to work out each morning because I have all these demands on my life, and I too like to watch Netflix and Chill, which is okay if you are married, by the way, or just watch a good sports game in the evening. Yes, I just said Netflix and Chill in my book. That is not a typo! I am married, so it's okay! Okay, back to the point here. Working out in the morning means that it is done! If I wait until my lunch hour or in the evening, there are too many things that get in the way that could potentially throw me off, so I just choose to make it a priority early in my day to avoid any issues. I have built my training programs around this principle, so our workout programs at my gyms start at 5 am. 80% of our training workouts are in the morning. That way, it gives people the opportunity to get it done early, and then they have the rest of the day to do all the things in life they have to do. Plus, you will feel amazing the whole day, which is awesome!

2. <u>Fat Burning</u>—Okay so what If I told you there was a way to stay lean year round, get rid of unwanted body fat, and feel great everyday. Would you want to know what it is? Of course you would and it is the reason why I work out early everyday. I work out early everyday to maximize the fat burning. Now there's a lot of science that backs this up, and some people will argue, but I am just telling you what works for me and so many of the people that I know that are fit. When you work out in the early morning hours on an empty stomach before eating, your body is generally in what we call a fasted state. What that means is since your last meal was probably the night before let's say 6 or 7 pm, by the time you wake up in the morning, your body has burned up the majority of its glycogen "Energy" while you were sleeping. How cool is that by the way, that while you sleep,

your body is burning calories! So now when you get up, have that cup of coffee while doing your Hour of Power, your body is burning fat for energy as you are sitting there. Now what most people do is they think they need to eat something right away because you know breakfast is the most important meal of the day right. Yes I would agree with that, but not for the reason you think. **Breakfast really just stands for Break-Fast. It is when you are breaking your fast.** The moment that you eat, basically begin to consume calories, or anything that turns your digestive system on, your body begins to burn that and not fat.

I am going to stay away from all the big science names or go into deep detail on this for now, but just know this is the way it works. The point of this section of the book is that you want to set your body up to burn fat for energy and not glycogen, or as I like to tell people, carbohydrates. So why do I work out in the morning? It's because I haven't eaten since the night before, and my body will be in fat-burning mode, not carbohydrate-burning mode. So, if your goal is to really set your body up to burn fat for fuel, which will help you get lean and stay lean, working out in the morning sets you up to do this in the most efficient way. If your body is already burning fat when you just sit there in the morning, doing your bible study, imagine what is going to happen if you go do 20-30 minutes of exercise. It is literally like throwing gas on the fire. Your body will burn fat like crazy! In the next chapter, I will go deeper into nutrition and intermittent fasting, which will give you more of the science of how this all works, but I want to stay on topic for now.

3. <u>Mental Victory</u>–The third reason why I work out early and would encourage you to do so is for the Mental Victory! Another way of saying it is that "you did it!" When we accomplish something and give ourselves credit for it, we get an immediate dopamine hit in the brain. Basically, it's a chemical that is released in your brain that makes you feel good! So when you knock out that workout early in the morning, not only do you flood your body with all these endorphins, but you also get dopamine as well because you followed through on doing something that you know is good for you! See, it really doesn't matter whether you workout out for 15 minutes, 30 minutes or even an hour. You did it, and you should reward yourself for following through. So I want to start my day off feeling great, knowing that I have already done what I needed to do. This builds self-confidence when we follow through on what we know we need to do and actually do it! Now you will be more prepared and confident for your day as you go into business meetings, etc. As I think about all the guys I know that are great businessmen and even women, all of them work out, and most of them work out early in the morning. All I can say is it works, and it will work for you!

CHAPTER 6

EATING FOR ENERGY

HOW FULL IS YOUR ENERGY TANK?

How full is your energy tank, my friend? Trust me when I say energy matters! It is a real thing, and it matters more than you think.

I will focus on energy from a nutrition standpoint in this chapter, but I want you to realize that energy is all around us. This is why I recommended you stay away from certain people that steal your energy earlier in the book. I was talking about mental energy there, but it is all the same. We need the energy to do everything we are required to do daily. So we have to be very mindful of what our Energy Tank looks like. Are we running on fumes each day, or are we full, feeling amazing?

We know how unhealthy it is to drive our cars around all day with the fuel light on low. If you do that too much, it can begin to create all kinds of underlying problems for the car. It certainly won't perform at its highest output. Then we have to think about what kind of gas we put in our cars. I know that two of the cars that we drive require premium fuel, not the cheap stuff. The reason is that they perform better, and the simple truth is that so does your body when you put what it needs in it. So in this chapter, I will be talking to you about Energy, How you can maximize your energy, and some things you can do from a Nutrition standpoint to really feel amazing!

INTERMITTENT FASTING

Okay, so before I start telling you about all the good foods that you should be putting in your body, which you probably already know, I want to talk to you about intermittent fasting and why I do it. There are many types of intermittent fasting, but the one that I am referring to and what I generally do is a 16/8 fast. All that really means is that I would prefer to fast for 16 hours without consuming any food and then eat within the 8-hour window. For me, that is generally 3–4 days a week, where I eat from 10 a.m.–6 p.m. or 11 a.m.-7 p.m. If you think about it, you're sleeping for 8 hours out of those 16 hours anyway, so it's not as hard as people would think. Once again, this book is all about what I have found to work for me best over the years and the many people I have personally helped. I have been in the fitness game for a long time now, tried every way of training and eating, and this is what I have found to be the best for multiple reasons.

In the last chapter, I shared with you why I chose to work out early. It is all about putting my body in a fat-burning zone. Now I want to go a little deeper into the science of this and not just talk about fat burning but some health benefits as well. See, as I have gotten older (currently, I am 40), I have looked for ways to look and feel better and, yes, you guessed it, have more energy! My old belief system before intermittent fasting and what I lived for years was to wake up and eat, and then eat basically all day long, six times a day or so. Then I started to learn more about intermittent fasting, and it really made a lot of sense to me. First, you must understand the amount of energy your digestive system demands to break down food, especially foods your body struggles to digest.

Like all the processed garbage in our foods today, such as grains, artificial sweeteners, etc. Most of these foods and drinks decrease our energy.

We create so much inflammation in our bodies, which we know is the root cause of pretty much every disease, and it leaves us feeling mentally and physically sluggish. So, as I began to learn more and more about the digestive system, it made sense to me that when I wasn't overwhelming my body with a constant workload of food to break down from the moment I woke up to the moment I went to bed, it could use that energy for something else. It is what I like to refer to as Energy Diversion. **Energy Diversion is where your body begins to use the same energy it would normally use to break down food to heal underlying issues.** This is powerful!

See If you wake up, and instead of eating right away, As I mentioned earlier, if you just drink water, your body can utilize fat for Energy versus Glycogen. The other thing that is happening without you knowing it is that your body has all this extra energy to heal since it doesn't have to work overtime to break down food. One of the first things that need healing is your gut. Now, if you don't know, your gut is where your immune system lives. So many people have gut problems, autoimmune diseases, bloating, and so on because the simple truth is that their gut can't keep up with the garbage that they are putting into it.

That is why I am such a big believer in not just intermittent fasting each day, but even prolonged fasting, where you might fast for 24 hours from dinner to dinner, just drinking water or coffee, to really give your body and gut a break. I like to do this once a month now. When I was healing my gut years ago, I would do it once a week. This helps clear out the garbage. Now you can do some things to help intensify fasting, and if you really want to look deep into this, I would encourage you to study some fasting experts like Dr. Jason Fung, Dr. Dan Pompa, or Dr. Josh Axe. Another great guy who is great when it comes to fasting is Thomas Delaurer. These guys can go really deep into the science of fasting. I even did a 5-day water fast about five years ago that was absolutely life-changing. I followed a protocol by Dr. Dan Pompa, and it was life-changing in more than one way. If you google Dr. Pompa's 5-Day Water Fast, you will find the one that I did. It is very detailed and explains all the benefits, what is to be expected, and so on. I will say this is not for everybody. You must not just jump into stuff like this without truly understanding how it all works. I studied this stuff for a long time before I did it.

Okay, once again, the point of intermittent fasting is all about energy! That is why I am telling you about this. When you really understand how the body utilizes energy, it makes sense. So when we are fasting, our body isn't using a massive amount of energy to break down food, and it can use fat to burn for fuel, keeping us lean while also utilizing energy to heal our body, especially the gut! So now that we are essentially conserving energy for what matters most, let's talk about how we can do some other things to keep our energy tanks full!

SUPER SHAKE TO THE RESCUE

One of the questions I get asked all the time is: What do I eat for breakfast? I think we have all heard that breakfast is the most important meal of the day. I would agree with that, but not because McDonald's or the cereal companies want me to believe that, but because of the importance of what I put in my body first when I break my fast. See, breakfast really stands for break-fast. What you eat first is going to break your fast, and we just talked about all the benefits of fasting. In this example, I want you to think about what you're putting into your body first. It really matters. Most people, when they break their fast in the morning, do it with a bowl of cereal, a pop tart, a breakfast sandwich from McDonald's, or whatever, and wonder why they don't have energy and feel like crap. That is why they need to get an energy drink to go along with it or coffee that is loaded with sugar to spike them up from the crash. This keeps them leveled out till lunch, and then they put some more garbage in their bodies, which requires a bunch of energy to break down, and they need another energy drink to stay level and get through the afternoon. This is the reality for too many people, by the way.

If you truly want to have great energy, it is so important that you start your day by loading your body with what it really needs, which is great nutrition. Something that is going to fuel you and give you energy versus demanding energy from you.

When you put the junk in, your body actually loses energy, whereas when you put the good stuff in, your body's energy tank rises.So here is what I have found that has worked best for me to help me start each day feeling amazing. It is what I like to refer to as my "Super Shake!" I am going to give you the exact ingredients of what I do every day to make it very simple for you. Trust me when I say this is a game-changer. If you make this one change in your lifestyle on a daily basis, you will absolutely feel amazing and better than before you started reading this book. This one thing could add years to your life.

Now, based on your size, you may want to increase or decrease the portion size of everything that you do. I am 6'1 and weigh 185, so this is perfect for me. I am looking to get about 600-700 calories in for my Super Shake, which I stay around 2000 to 2500 calories a day. I am focused on getting a good blend of protein, clean carbs, good fats, and fruits and vegetables in this shake, which are all needed for a multitude of reasons to support a healthy body that is full of energy. I consume this shake in the morning after I work out because, remember, I like to work out while fasting so that my body is burning fat for energy.

I do consume some Essential Amino Acids before my workout to protect my muscles from breaking down and being used for energy, but I don't consume any food. So by the time I get my weight training workout done, I am ready for this Super Shake, and I can literally feel it flooding my body and cells, instantly giving me the nutrition I need for recovery, muscle repair, and, yes, energy. As I shared with you earlier, I extend my fast on days that I only do cardio and drink the shake around 11, and on the days I lift, I consume it a little earlier in the day, like around 9:30. This is why I love making this shake in a Nutribullet because on the days that I am not breaking my fast till around 11; I can just make it in the morning while I'm making the kids' breakfast and just put it in the fridge. I can take it to my office with me or leave it in the fridge until I'm ready for it.

It literally takes 2-3 minutes to make, and I am ready to go. Okay, so now you know all the reasons why I believe in this Super Shake, but I'm sure you want to know that magic formula. Here it is!

Super Shake Recipe

32 ozNutribullet Cup—Invest in a Nutribullet! It is a game changer!

Here is the order that I make it and what I put in it.

16 oz of Unsweetened Vanilla Almond milk—No sugar or junk dairy

A Handful of Spinach pressed down to the bottom—This gives you room for everything else!—Veggies

⅓ banana and ½ cup of frozen blueberries—Fruits

¼ frozen Avocado, ½ tablespoon of Natural PB or Almond Butter—Good Fats

30 grams of Clean Grass Fed Whey Protein, Bone Broth, or Plant-Based Protein Powder. Many times I will mix all 3 sources together!—Protein

There it is! I simply mix all this into the 32oz Nutribullet cup, add some water to get a little above the max line, and mix it up. I then drink it pretty much immediately if it's after a weight training workout, and on my cardio days, I will take it to work with me and drink it a little later in the morning. As I was saying earlier, I don't believe that breakfast is the most important meal of the day because of the time, but more because of what you put in your body. The first thing to break your fast is what matters. As you can see, with this shake, I am flooding my body with all kinds of great nutrients that my body thrives on. I have included every food group in this shake that you need, from protein to help build and repair muscles, Carbs for energy, Good Fats, which promote great brain and heart health, and Fruits and Veggies, which we know have so many benefits.

As soon as I drink this shake, I immediately feel amazing. This, along with quality supplements like a good multivitamin/multimineral, Probiotic, and Fish Oil, and I am ready to go! I do some other products like green powders, Vitamin D, pre-workouts, etc.

Trust me, friend, If you commit to starting your day with this Super Shake, you will feel absolutely amazing!

YOU ARE WHAT YOU EAT!

Alright, as we begin to land the plane on the fitness component of this book, I want to remind you of something. You are the best investment you can ever make. You are going to hear me say that a lot! Does it cost money to take care of your health? Yes, of course, it does. I would really prefer to think of it as an investment. **The truth is that you will either pay now or pay later when it comes to investing in your health.** Every day, you make decisions about what you put into your body. Do I eat the salad before dinner or the dessert after? I'm not gonna lie; sometimes I do both, but if I am committed to a program and working towards a goal, I know I need to have the salad, which helps me get full along with the main course, and now I'm not hungry and have no room for dessert. If I skip the salad or extra veggies, now I feel I have the room, and boom, I say bring me the dessert. These decisions I make daily add up over time. So the way I teach nutrition is to figure out the foods that you like and that are actually good for you and stick to those foods 90% of the time. I am not eating food to be satisfied or to help with some emotional problems. **I am eating food for fuel. I want the benefits of the nutrition I am putting into my body to give me energy for the day.** It really is about your mindset when it comes to food and nutrition. Some people might think it's expensive to eat well, buy organic fruits and vegetables, almond milk vs. cheap milk, or organic grass-fed meat vs. cheap stuff. I will just generally ask people if they are willing to give up the money they are spending on junk like sweets, cigarettes, and eating out and invest that same amount of money on eating higher-quality foods. It really is an exchange system, my friend. You are no longer spending money on junk that is killing you and investing in foods and supplements that are helping you add Energy, Vitality, and Years of quality of life. I would say that rates pretty far up there on the investment scale!

I am not going to go into a full-out nutrition program here, but what I am going to do is give you some options that I believe would be great for you to choose from and a simple nutrition guide that you can use. If you will take a second to look for foods that you actually like, select them, and then build your day around them. Now I am a big fan of eating my carbs earlier in the day so that my body can burn through them, so as I sleep at night and stay fasting the next morning, my body is burning fat.

Here is a list of the sources I like to use for my Protein, Carbs, and Fats:

Protein: Organic Chicken, Grass Fed Beef, Free Range Eggs, Wild Caught Salmon, Greek Yogurt and Protein Powders like Bone Broth Protein, Grass Fed Whey, and Plant based.

Carbs: Sweet Potatoes, Oats, Rice, for my Complex Carbs, Berries, Apples, Bananas, Grapefruit for my Fruits, and Spinach, Kale, Broccoli, Brussel Sprouts, and Leafy Green Salad Mix for my Veggies.

Fats: Coconut Oil, Ghee Butter, Grass Fed Butter, Avocados, Natural PB or Almond Butter, Almonds, Macadamia Nuts, Walnuts.

The foods that I have listed above are pretty much what I eat on a daily/weekly basis. I could list a lot more, but what I have found that works best is to keep it simple. I start each day with a Super Shake, have a lunch filled with Protein, Clean Carbs, and Veggies, and then dinner is more of a Protein, Veggies, and Fat. As I said before, I tend to cut out the carbs later in the day, especially the slow burners. I will mix in a protein shake in between lunch and dinner if I feel like I need an extra meal or if I am having a late dinner sometimes just to hold me over so that when I get home, I'm not raiding the pantry eating anything, I can find which are usually food or snacks that are or good for me.

The best way to have success with this diet is to actually do it. Nutrition really isn't rocket science. It really comes down to self-discipline. **Self-discipline is doing what you know you should do, even when you don't feel like doing it.** So we know we should exercise, eat quality foods like the ones I have listed in this book, and take good supplements. It really just boils down to doing it. Now that is why I have recommended hiring a coach or trainer multiple times already in this book because many of us know what to do, but we need the extra accountability, which is fine. I have had coaches for over a decade now in almost every area of my life. **A coach is not a crutch but a Champion!**

A champion is somebody who fights on behalf of you towards a goal. As you are working hard every day to be the Champion that God created you to be, trust me when I say you should always have somebody in your corner helping Champion you in the process of achieving that goal. There is a saying: if you want to go fast, go alone; if you want to go far, go together. We all need that extra support from somebody with us, loving, encouraging, and empowering us. That is why I have always invested in a coach, and I am a coach. I love to be that Champion for somebody, whether it's helping them grow in their faith, marriage, business, or in this case, better their health!

SHOULD I USE SUPPLEMENTS?

Now that we have dialed in the right foods we are going to eat on a daily basis to support our exercise program and help the body have an abundance of energy, let's talk about something I get asked about all the time. What supplements should I take? I hear this question all the time, friends. First, let me tell you how I feel about supplements. They are called supplements because they are meant to supplement an already good nutrition program. Meaning bridge the gap if you will.

So I don't believe in any magic pill, powder, or potion. The truth is that you are going to have to do the work. Exercise and eating for energy are going to come first in this equation. Once you begin to exercise daily and eat for energy, supplements can really add a tremendous amount of value to your daily routine of feeling amazing.

Before I go into what I take or recommend, I will say again that this is what I have found that has worked for many people I know and me. I am not a doctor or your nutritionist. I am just a guy who has studied exercise, nutrition, and longevity with a passion for over 20 years now and has been the guinea pig over those years. When I find something that works, I stick with it. I always look to improve, feel, and perform better.

Here are the top supplements that I would recommend using daily and why!

MultiVitamin/MultiMineral- 92% of the U.S. population at the time of this writing has some type of vitamin or mineral deficiency. There are many reasons for this, like poor soil used for farming, processed foods that rob our bodies of vitamins and minerals, and insufficient sunlight.

Probiotics–As I have said multiple times, your gut is where your immune system lives. Most people's guts have been compromised by toxins, too many grains that are hard to digest, stress, inflammatory foods like processed foods, animal protein loaded with hormones, etc. Probiotics help to restore the gut microbiome, create healthy bacteria, and, most importantly, boost your immune system.

Fish Oil/Krill Oil- Simply put, most people don't get anywhere near the amount of good fat their body needs. Actually, most people are loaded up with too many unhealthy fats. When you understand the benefits of good fats and what they do for your body, it really will change your perspective. I am not personally saying go keto here. Still, I will say that I believe having way more fats in your diet, along with supplementing them in, is better than loading your body with crappy carbs like sugar, sweets, or even many grains that cause inflammation. The fact is that your body, actually every cell, is surrounded by what is called a lipid bilayer. The health of a cell has a lot to do with your being able to get good stuff in and the bad stuff out. Without going into ATP, how your cells produce energy, basically, just know, when you are eating the right balance of fats, your body will definitely thank you! If you want to know more about what the right balance is, I would encourage you to Google Dr. Josh Axe. You can get your fat from different things, but once again, if you're coming up short and you need to bridge the gap, you can use quality fish oil or krill oil.

Vitamin D–I live in Ohio, so this is something that I have to use. We don't get even close to the amount of sun year round that we need, so I must supplement with some extra Vitamin D. The benefits are promoting healthy bones and teeth, supporting immune, brain, and nervous system health, regulating insulin levels, and so much more.

Greens Powder–Yes, I do a Greens Powder pretty much every day! I know the power of all these good ingredients like wheat grass, kale, and spinach, but I don't really enjoy eating all that in a big bowl, so I just use a green powder. This is super alkalizing for your body, and you feel absolutely amazing. It helps boost the immune system and digestion and once again keeps your body in an alkaline state, which is shown to reduce cancer as cancer thrives in a highly acidic environment. I have tried a lot of Greens powders over the years and by far the best I have ever used and still use is my brother Steve Weatherford's product by Veritas Labs. You can Google Steve or Veritas Labs to find it. It is awesome and tastes amazing!

Clean Protein Powders–This I could talk about all day, but I will keep it simple. You need more protein in your diet, and sometimes eating a steak, chicken breast, or scrambled eggs isn't always convenient. This is why I start each day with a protein shake, AKA Super Shake, and often do a second one in the afternoon between lunch and dinner. Not a super shake, but a ready-to-drink shake. We need protein to help build and repair muscles, ligaments, and tendons. It helps build lean muscle and ultimately burns body fat. The biggest thing with Protein Powders is that you have to really watch what you're buying. There is so much junk out there that is filled with artificial sweeteners like sucralose that destroys your gut, messes with your hormones, and many other things that are detrimental to your overall health. I won't go into all that you don't want because we could be here all day. I will just say that what I am looking for is a good Grass Fed Protein, Non-GMO, No Added Hormones, No added sugars, or especially artificial sugars, and ideally tested through NSF or Informed Choice. I personally use stuff from ID Life, Garden of Life, Ancient Nutrition, or OWYN. The Ready To Go meal replacement shakes are easy and convenient. I generally have the Whey Protein after my workouts with some collagen protein, and on the days I do just cardio, I tend to stick to a plant-based protein with some added collagen in my shakes.

This is just what I have found that works for me. I have gone into some deep detail here with this because, over the years, I have seen many people be very overwhelmed with what to take.

You can get lost in the supplement aisle these days. Years ago, you would have had to go to a GNC to get your supplements, but now every retail store, grocery outlet, or even drugstore has an aisle for supplements. I hope this helps make it easy for you to get what you need and, most importantly, get started! Most people get paralysis by analysis because they don't know where to begin, so they never get started. This should make it easy to get going!

Okay, just a few more things I have found to help me, and we will close out this chapter and keep moving! I'm not going into deep detail, but I do believe in some other things that I mix into my nutrition, like bone broth for gut health, Dr. Pompa's True Cellular Detox program every January for proper cellular cleansing, and last but not least, I drink a lot of clean water. I have a reverse osmosis system with an alkaline filter under my kitchen sink. We try to avoid drinking tap water as we know it is loaded with all kinds of junk like fluoride and chlorine.

So now you have the knowledge you need when it comes to exercise and nutrition to go to the next level in your health and fitness. In the next chapter, I will go deeper into the third component that I think is crucial to you living your best life and feeling amazing each day. That third component is RECOVERY!

CHAPTER 7

RECOVERY MATTERS

The last thing that I want to go into quickly is the things that I do on a daily, weekly, or monthly basis for recovery. **I truly believe that true Wealth begins with Health.** That is why I am talking about things like exercise, nutrition, and recovery first in this book. We will get to the financial part here soon, but first, I want to make sure that you are doing things in the right order. The financial aspect is crucial as it will give you the resources to do all these things I am about to cover, so they go hand in hand.

So there are a million things that you can do to help take care of your body. I'm sure you always see ads on TV, social media, etc. You can spend tens of thousands on stem cell therapy, exotic wellness spas, specialized treatments, and doctors. If you have that kind of money, great, but to be honest, you don't need it. I will give you five things that I think are crucial that don't take much time or money at all at the end of the day. I have already covered some, so I won't go into much detail here as I already have. Once again, this book is all about sharing with you what I have found that has worked for the many people I have had the privilege of coaching over the years and me. You will never know until you give them a try. So here are my top 5.

1. Chiropractic Care–I am a huge believer in Chiropractic Care. Our chiropractor, Dr. Juan Fernandez, at Full Life Chiropractic in Troy, Ohio, is our doctor. I can do everything I need through him. He can order blood tests, refer if needed, and so on. Now I will say we believe more in Corrective Care than just going to a normal chiropractor. I have some very close friends who are chiropractors, and what is really funny is that pretty much all of my friends that I know or follow are in great shape. I will just tell you that one of the big reasons my family and I regularly get adjusted is because I understand how the body works. Your spine is the core of all of your body's functions. The spine is a key element in optimal health as it protects your central nervous system—the system that connects your entire body, helping it to communicate and react to daily factors. Improper spinal alignment is common and can be caused by both physical and emotional challenges. Spinal misalignment diminishes nerve supply and weakens the body. Aligning your spine and correcting abnormalities caused by stress or injury maximizes your nerve supply and clears pathways to optimize wellness. Enhancing nerve supply through spinal correction allows the body's systems to naturally interact and integrate without interference.

2. Infrared Sauna–I am a huge believer in using an Infrared Sauna at least 1-2 times a week. The simple truth here is that our bodies are being inundated with different toxins daily from the environment, food, household cleaners, etc. So, sitting in the sauna allows me to sweat out many of these toxins on a weekly basis while I also receive the other benefits of the sauna. Here are just a couple of them, and I use a Sunlighten

Sauna just because it is proven to have the lowest EMFs, which I want to stay away from. The sauna is great for relaxation, detoxification, weight loss, relief from sore muscles, joint pain, and improving circulation, and it will definitely help you with sleep.

3. Rebounding–Okay, you guys may immediately think about playing basketball here, but that is not the type of rebounding that I mean. What I am referring to here is simply jumping on a mini trampoline, or what is referred to as rebounding. This is something that is so beneficial for your overall health and extremely helpful in helping the body remove waste and toxins from the body. I generally prefer to rebound for 10 minutes a day before I go into my Infrared Sauna. Since your lymphatic system doesn't have a pump like your circulatory system does, rebounding helps aid in moving toxins out of your body. The last thing you want is waste and toxins to be stagnant in your body, just like water that sets and can't run into other channels of water. Eventually, you will know what that water looks like. Now imagine that inside your body. After all, we are made up of over 70% water. I am all about doing anything I can to remove toxins from my body. This is a great way to do that and enjoy all the other health benefits of rebounding. It is great for overall heart health, strengthening your immune system, being easy on your joints, effective calorie burning, and it's fun!

4. Personal Care Products, Household Cleaners, and WIFI -Speaking of removing toxins and how rebounding does that. Now I want to cover how to stop overloading your body with toxins so that you're not overburdened to begin with. Many people

are aware of food toxins and why it's important to eat organic, but one thing I wasn't aware of was the number of toxins in things like personal care products, household cleaners, and Wi-Fi. The truth is if you want to feel amazing and have great health, you have to be aware of what is going into your body on all levels. **Most of our shampoos, conditioners, body washes, face washes, deodorant, and make-up are loaded with toxic chemicals that you really want to stay away from.** These things have stuff like aluminum, sulfates, parabens, and other toxic chemicals that are wrecking people's nervous systems, guts, etc. So I would highly encourage you to be mindful of what products and go all natural. Anything that goes on your skin or that you consume is so important. Cleaning products are important as well. Laundry detergent, dishwashing, hand soap. You really have to watch it all. Last on this list is Wi-Fi. I am not going to go deep into detail here on Wi-Fi, but just know that the EMFs from things like your cell phone, ear pods, and Wi-Fi in your home are things you need to be aware of. Do your own research. So my solution to all of this is to use clean products. We have made that switch over the last 4-5 years and will never go back. In my opinion, all this stuff matters for your long-term health in my opinion. It really isn't that much more expensive, and it gives me peace of mind.

5. Cold Showers—Okay, the last thing I want to cover as far as recovery and overall health is cold showers! There are some massive benefits to cold therapy. We know that the big one is reducing inflammation. Inflammation is the root cause of all diseases. Every time we put something foreign in our bodies, our

bodies have an inflammatory response. This is a good thing. However, we don't want our bodies to always be working overtime around the clock. This is why we want to get rid of all the chemicals we have been putting in our bodies through foods, personal care products, and household cleaners.

... So, anyhow, here is why I love cold showers. First, they are free! You can buy a cold plunge, go to a cryotherapy chamber, and do other stuff, which are all great. However, if you don't have those resources, I know you have cold water that comes out of your shower. If you have ever been so poor to have had your gas or electricity turned off, and your hot water heater didn't work, you have already experienced this! By the way, that is not the best way to experience this, but I have been there before. Anyhow, taking a cold shower, or at least starting your shower, by stepping into the cold for the first 30 seconds and then turning the water to warm, is a mind and body experience at the same time. The first thing is that you are training yourself to do something that is uncomfortable. I don't care how many times I have taken a cold shower, which is pretty much every day; I never really look forward to it. However, daily it trains me to do something that I don't really want to do, which builds me stronger mentally. Now it does help to know that there are a ton of benefits and that I know it is truly benefiting my body and overall health. Even with that said, it still sucks at times.

So as I step into the cold water, feeling the initial shock of the cold, it gives me the chance to just breathe. In my opinion, this is simulating adversity. It is super uncomfortable, and more than likely, you will face situations like this in your life. This is a training ground for me. Cold showers and ice baths are super uncomfortable in those initial 30 seconds, so you have to be able to breathe, gather yourself, and just relax. This is exactly what you need to do in times of stress. This cold initially stresses the body, but it is good stress because it prepares you to deal with stress in your life. It is why we exercise. We are stressing the body, but at the same time preparing it and making it more fit and stronger! I firmly believe that if you can get yourself to do this, you can get yourself to do darn near anything. So yes, this is a mental thing, but there are a ton of benefits from a recovery standpoint. Cold showers reduce inflammation, improve circulation, boost the immune system, improve alertness, help the body handle daily stress, and so much more. So here is your challenge! Next time you step into the shower, let the water run cold, step into it for 30 seconds and just breathe. Do a couple of slow turns and let the cold water just hit you as you breathe and think about what a Champion you are. This is an absolutely freeing feeling, and you will feel like a bad a$$! After 30 seconds, go ahead and go warm for 30 seconds, and then take your regular shower temperature, being self-aware of what you just did and all the benefits your body just got from your boldness. Are you up for the challenge? I know you can do it!

As you can see here, I have a true passion for this kind of stuff. For many years, it was just more about basic Exercise, Nutrition, and Recovery. Then there was a series of events that happened in my life that turned my world upside down. Before I move on to the next section of this book, I feel now would be a good time to share with you the story that really set me on the path of being so passionate about my health and learning to not just follow the crowd. What I'm about to share with you is 100% why I am so passionate about my health and appreciate my life more today than ever before.

CHAPTER 8

MY BATTLE WITH MERCURY POISON

I didn't know much about all this extra health stuff until I got mercury poisoning from silver fillings in my teeth and became really sick. I had to become a master at doing everything I could to help my body feel great. The basics are exercise, eating right, and taking supplements. What I experienced with Mercury Poisoning put a whole new emphasis on everything I talked about in this book. I had to learn how to become a master at setting my body up to heal and, most importantly, how to get rid of the poison that was in my body, wrecking my life. Actually, let me tell you the story here real quick. It may end up helping you or somebody you know, as many people who are sick today are being told it's one thing when there is a way deeper issue.

I have always been very healthy as a kid and as an adult. I worked out, I was physically in good shape, and I ate decently, other than consuming probably way too much sugar, I must admit. Long story short, though, I have never had any health problems. So in September of 2011, I was feeling amazing, living life, and everything was going awesome. I was growing in my faith; my marriage was getting better daily; we had a new business that was really taking off. Life was going amazing! Then a turn of events happened that would set me on a journey for the next three years of my life that was a wild ride. It all started on Labor Day 2011 when I went to visit one of my close friends and business partner, Skip Jackson, at his work. Skip was such an incredible man who had become a close friend, one of my training clients, and a business partner. I loved spending time with him, driving to different meetings, talking about life, and envisioning the future. He would sometimes make me laugh so hard that my cheeks would be sore the next day. We worked really well together and had a tremendous amount of fun!

On that day, labor day, as I pulled up to Skip's office to visit him, there was a police car parked out front. I can remember pulling up to the office, rolling down my window in my car, and asking the officer if everything was okay. He said yes. I said, "Oh, okay, great." Then I asked, "Is Skip inside?" He answered, "Yes," and then these words that I still have trouble saying to this day. He said, "Mr. Jackson is deceased. At that time, I believe I had the first anxiety attack of my life. I was in shock, and I had never been taught how to really handle that. He was the first person really close to me that I had ever lost in my life. Up until this point, at 32 years old, I had never lost a parent, close family member, or friend. This was a tipping point for me and my health, which is why I'm sharing this story. For the next couple of weeks, I struggled with some panic attacks, and I had no idea what was going on. I thought it just had to do with what happened with Skip.

So my wife and I thought it would be a good idea to take a trip to Mexico for a week just to get away and relax. We loved to travel, and all-inclusive trips were always a great way to just "get away." But things got even worse while we were in Mexico for the week. I could not shake this anxiety. My mind and body were freaking out. I thought I was having a heart attack and was going to die, so we rushed to the closest Mexican hospital to get me checked out. When we arrived, there was literally a receptionist, a nurse, and a doctor. It was the most bizarre thing ever. We told them what was going on, and they immediately began to run all kinds of tests on me, hooking me up to all these machines, etc. Then, about an hour later, they came in, showed us x-rays, and began to tell us I had an enlarged heart. As you can imagine, I was freaking out.

To make matters worse, nobody spoke English, so my wife was literally communicating back and forth through some translation app on her phone. Just telling this story here in the book brings back this crazy event in my mind. They shot me up with all kinds of drugs that day and then wouldn't let us leave until we paid the bill. When they said it was 15,000 pesos, I freaked out! I thought I was never going to leave this hospital. Luckily, that was only $1100 in American money.

Once we got back to the resort, I was out of it. I think I slept for 24 hours. My poor wife had to deal with me, and I knew I was acting crazy. I wish I could tell you it got better after this, but it didn't. I wanted to fly home immediately to get checked, and Rachel was like, "no way. We are staying and relaxing. We didn't come all the way here just to fly home." She was very adamant that I was fine. "There is nothing wrong with you, Curt," she kept telling me. So I was a zombie on the beach for the next two days. As we traveled back home, the flying was crazy. I mismarked every question on the immigration form, basically saying we were bringing all kinds of animals, money, and illegal things with us back into the country, so we got detained for that, which really got my wife fired up. The Mexican authorities looked at us like we were terrorists. So now, every time we travel, even ten years later, I'm still not allowed to fill out the immigration card!

Okay, so we got home, and yes, the first thing I did was go to the emergency room to get checked out. I was still having anxiety, panic attacks, and so on. I got checked out, and they told me I was fine. My heart looked good, my blood work was fine, and it was just anxiety that I should just get on some anxiety medication, work out, maybe meditate or do yoga, and I would be good. So that is what I did. They just thought it was stress. Now, I will tell you that I have always taken supplements, but I am not a big believer in medications. As a believer and a person that knows how to control their mindset, I thought I would be able to beat all this anxiety with my faith and manage my mindset. The only thing was that there was a deeper issue than just some past traumas or future events that I was worried about.

So, as the story evolves, the next two years of my life were the most difficult ones I have ever been through. My health continued to decline. I had headaches daily, ringing in my ears, brain fog, light sensitivity, neurological issues, burning in my legs and tingling, and so much more. I probably had three to four emergency room visits. I consulted every specialist I could find, from a heart specialist doing stress tests to a neurologist doing two brain MRIs, a rheumatologist, multiple blood tests, etc. I was living in hell, and really nobody knew what was going on. My wife thought I was crazy, and I was. At one point, I was on so many drugs, from Zoloft to Vicodin for the pain, Valium for sleep, Risperdal, an antipsychotic drug, and some other stuff. I couldn't sleep no matter what I took and began to have suicidal thoughts. I couldn't work, my wife couldn't leave me alone, and it took a toll on our family.

I can remember the day I walked down to my office in the basement to check our life insurance policies. This was the day that I was going to go to Walmart, purchase a gun, and end this hell I was living in. I couldn't take it anymore. As I looked at our policies, we were two months away from the Suicidal clause, which basically said that if I died from suicide, my family would get nothing. I am almost 100% certain that if I hadn't checked that policy that day, I would not be here writing this book. There was no way I could check out like that and leave my family. Just a few days later, I made an appointment with a physiatrist that my mentor recommended. On the morning of this appointment, my wife and I had a massive fight after I held a kitchen knife to my throat. I was so lost. I can remember a few minutes later hearing my wife talk to somebody on the phone in the basement and just hearing her cry out and tell this person, "I just want my husband back." I sat there on the stairs sobbing as I wanted the same thing. I just wanted my life back. I wanted to be the Husband, Father, and Leader that I had envisioned myself to be. That morning, Dr. Ange realized the doctors had me on too many medications that were really messing me up. She was able to get me somewhat leveled out, which ultimately bought me some time. That $500 1 hour visit that I didn't want to go to, saved my life. I met with her every month, and although my life was getting better, I still had all the symptoms of mercury poisoning, but at least I wasn't suicidal. I was still in a ton of pain and still on a bunch of meds, but I was able to continue my search for a solution. I was not willing to just accept the doctors' telling me it was a possible autoimmune issue, anxiety, or that I was fine. I knew I wasn't fine.

In October of 2014, I went to a Tony Robbins Unleash the Power event in Dallas, Texas, and while I was there, I got absolute certainty that I would find a solution. Throughout these two years, I continued to pray daily for God to give me an answer. I would spend many sleepless nights in my closet reading the Bible, praying, journaling, and trying to figure out what was happening. I knew that my healing would come. So I went to this conference in Dallas and visited a church on that Sunday before we flew home that Danny McDaniel led called Bethel Dallas. That day, Cody Mahon prayed for healing over me, and my belief that I would find my healing went to another level.

On the flight home that day, my bible verse for my devotion was **Jeremiah 33:3, which says, "Call to me and I will answer you and tell you great and unsearchable things you do not know."** I also wrote down Jeremiah 33:6, which says, "Nevertheless, I will bring health and healing to it; I will heal people and let them enjoy abundant peace and security." See, as I wrote down those passages, I believed that my answer to unsearchable things and my healing would come. One thing I can tell you is that throughout this 2-year journey, I always believed. I'm not going to say I never doubted or became discouraged because I did. However, I stayed close to God, asking the Holy Spirit for strength every day and the courage to keep going. Well, friends, my healing was on the way! God was about to deliver me from all of this.

That next Friday, as I was searching and praying, God gave me the idea to call an old friend. Rachel Axe, the sister of Dr. Josh Axe, who, in my opinion, is one of the best Health Advocates in the world today, just so happened to be a friend of mine. I thought if anybody could help me, it would be Josh. So I called Rachel and began to explain to her what had happened to me over the past two years. All the doctors' visits, medications, symptoms, etc. We were on the phone for less than 5 minutes when she cut me off. What she said next literally revealed the unsearchable thing I was looking for. She said, "Curt, do you have silver fillings?" I thought that was a weird question, and no other doctor of the 50 I had seen in the last two years had asked me that. I said, "Yes, I have a whole mouth full of them, 11 to be exact," and then she said it. **"You have Mercury Poisoning."** Boom, there was the answer I was looking for. Now at first, I was like, "Rachel, there is no way. I don't know much about Mercury poisoning, but I do know that I had every blood test you could ever get done, about 4 or 5 times over the past two years, and every test had been perfect." I told her that, and she began to explain to me how silver fillings, or what is called amalgam fillings, were loaded with mercury and how they, over the years, leak out mercury into your mouth, which then heads into your gut and brain, bypassing the blood-brain barrier and attack your nervous system, causing all kinds of problems. Every symptom I had experienced was right on with this. I was literally dealing with heavy metal poisoning all along. That phone call changed my life and gave me so much hope!

LET THE HEALING PROCESS BEGIN

I had hope now, but there was still a lot of work to be done. I had some serious poison in my body that was wrecking my life. As I began researching this, I came across a doctor named Dr. Pompa, who had experienced the same issues as I had. He was a Chiropractor who dealt with his own journey of heavy metal poisoning after years of being debilitated from it. Through his journey, he not only became well but became one of the leading doctors in the world on heavy metal detoxification. So I knew he was the guy to try to contact to help me with this. I wrote him an email, and within a couple of days, he responded. One thing I have learned in life is when it comes to your health, don't go cheap. I didn't want just any doctor helping me with this. I wanted somebody who knew exactly what was going on, who had experienced my exact situation, and I found Dr. Pompa.

Over the next couple of months, we began the process of truly understanding what was going on with my brain and body. I learned so much from him about detox, the body all the way down to the cellular level, and I had hope for the first time in years. Now, I must be honest; through all this mess, we were struggling financially, so that was still a challenge. However, when you're desperate, you take desperate measures. I took out a zero percent credit card to pay the $7000 to hire Dr. Pompa for the 6-month program to help me detox and also to pay the $3000 to remove the 11 silver fillings I had in my mouth. This was just the beginning, as there were still different supplements that I had to purchase, the need for an infrared sauna, and other things. It didn't matter to me; I just wanted my health back. I wish I could say everything went perfectly, but detoxing mercury out of your brain isn't sunshine and rainbows. Some days were extremely difficult, and I felt sick as could be. It really was a learning process and a journey. It took me about two years of detoxing to really get back to about 95%. Now seven years later, after all this, I still do body and brain cleanses at the start of every year to reduce the burden of heavy metals in my system, along with a few other things. I would consider myself 100% today, and I have fully recovered from what was probably the most difficult challenge I have ever had to endure in my life. **One of the greatest gifts I received from this time of my life is the gift of Gratitude. I appreciate my life more than ever today. Especially my Health!**

Maybe you have been through something like this or know somebody that has. You have overcome a major sickness or disease. Maybe it was a financial demise or a nasty divorce. Nobody ever wants to go through things like this, but they are, in fact, part of life. All I know is every time I go through something difficult; it makes me stronger. Once again, I wanted to share my story of Mercury poisoning with you for two reasons. Number one, you may be dealing with something similar right now or know somebody with some major health issues, and they could be dealing with some type of heavy metal poisoning, breast implant illness, mold, or something unconventional. This could potentially be an answer for you or them. The second reason I wanted to share this with you was to tell you why I am so passionate about my approach to health with Exercise, Nutrition, and Recovery. Things like fasting, infrared sauna, rebounding, detoxing, cutting out artificial sweeteners, personal care products loaded with chemicals like sulfates, and other approaches I have realized are huge difference makers in your health.

TRUE WEALTH IS HEALTH

As I close this section of the book, I want you to be self-aware of something. The truth is living a Champion Life and becoming the Champion leader that God has created you to be; living out your Purpose and Mission here on earth is going to require you to be around. So many people don't truly take the time to think about how important their overall health is. As an Entrepreneur, I think about wealth and money a lot. With that being said, I can tell you right now that **True Wealth starts with your Health.** I know I have talked a lot about that in this book; actually, I went deeper into this than I originally planned, but It is just what I feel is so important in being able to live your life to the fullest. If you don't have your health, all the money in the world isn't going to matter. There is a saying, "Man sacrifices his health in order to make money; then he sacrifices money to recuperate his health." I think it's best to just be proactive and get it right from the beginning. Put your overall fitness and health first. Then you will be able to have more energy, feel better, and hopefully get more time on this earth to do the things you love to do.

As you can see, I have talked a lot about Faith and Fitness so far in this book. Those have come first because I believe they are foundational to the other focuses I will begin to get into in the next chapter, which is Family and Finances. I live by what I like to call my 5 F- Focus. They are Faith, Fitness, Family, Finances, and Fun. **The 5 F-Focuses help me execute each day and take care of the most important things in my life**. I believe faith is foundational for so many reasons, which I have already explained. Then Fitness, your Mental, Emotional, and Physical are next. If you don't take care of yourself, it is going to be hard to be the best for your family or business/profession. So I hope that what I have covered so far has added value to your life, helping you to become better in these areas. That is the purpose and intent of this book. To share with you things that have blessed my life and helped me live a better life. So now that we have these foundations in place let's start to talk about what it looks like to have an incredible family life and create financial freedom. That is what is coming up next!

CHAPTER 9

BE THE CEO OF YOUR FAMILY

I have had the pleasure of being a coach many times in my life. It started with getting the opportunity to coach my kids in tee ball. If you have ever had the opportunity to coach tee ball with a bunch of little 5-year-olds running around, playing in the dirt, staring at the planes flying in the sky while you're trying to get them to focus on catching the ball, it can be interesting. I have also had the opportunity to coach many men about life, leadership, and business. So that is quite a scale, from 5-year-old kids to grown men looking to level up as husbands, fathers, and leaders. One of the things that I believe in wholeheartedly is the importance of the family unit. I refer to my family many times as "Team Tucker." We have a way of being, called the Tucker Family Way, which I will share with you here in a second. I have coached many people and many teams, but my home team, Team Tucker, will be the greatest coaching opportunity I will ever be given. God has blessed me with my wife, Rachel, and our four kids, Mariah, Austin, Carson, and Carli. Every day, this team is counting on me to lead from the front, creating a game plan for success that ensures that we experience victory as much as possible.

One of the greatest roles that I get to play as the Head Coach of Team Tucker is being the CEO. In a business, the CEO is the leader of the business. He or she calls the shots, leads the organization, and is responsible for the success and profitability of the business. He or she is the Chief Executive Officer. I am not talking about that type of CEO, even though as the leader of my home, I am responsible for all of those roles, I guess you could say. I am referring more to the CEO, meaning Chief Encouragement Officer for your family. I believe encouragement is life for the soul. It is my job to constantly breathe life into the spirit of my wife and kids, to let them know how much I love them, how proud I am of them, and that they know they can do anything they set their minds to. Also, I want them to know that they can count on me to be there to help them with whatever it is that they want to do. I have said over and over that my mission and purpose in life is to Love, Encourage, and Empower people to become the Champion Leaders that God has created them to be. Well, this starts at home with my wife and kids. They are my number-one ministry!

Too many times, you see people give their best to their jobs, church, or whatever, and their family gets their leftovers. This is a recipe for disaster or at least divorce. In this section of this Champion Life Playbook, I want to give you some practical things that I have implemented into my marriage and family life that have taken my wife and me from being on the verge of a divorce to literally having a marriage that is filled with so much passion, peace, and intimacy on all levels. Also, our family unit is stronger than ever, and we are experiencing victory in so many ways. I always tell the guys I coach that if you make millions of dollars and in the process end up divorced and your kids don't know who you are, that is not success. That, in my opinion, would be the ultimate failure.

MAKING YOUR MARRIAGE A PRIORITY

One of my favorite Proverbs out of the Bible is Proverbs 31:10-12, which says, "A wife of noble character who can find? She is worth far more than rubies. 11. Her husband has full confidence in her and lacks nothing of value. 12. She brings him good, not harm, all the days of her life. "When I read this proverb, it is a reminder to me of the blessing that Rachel is in my life. See, if I can be honest, in our early years, I didn't see Rachel the way I see her today. For many years, I was a very selfish man, as I have already explained, and our marriage was far more about what she could do for me than approaching it from a servant-spouse mindset. I didn't truly know her value to me. Not in terms of what she could do for me, but from the perspective of how much she was worth. Rachel is one of the greatest gifts that I have ever received in my life.

I'm sure you probably have something that somebody gave you at some point in your life, maybe as a kid, a baseball card, doll, car, or whatever, and you put it away in a safe space. Basically, you did that to protect it. You don't want anything to happen to it because it means a lot to you. Sadly, I have to say that many people will treat their car, set of golf clubs, or maybe a certain friend with more love and affection than their spouse. Then they wonder why there are eventually issues in their marriage. You could say that is what leads couples to lose that loving feeling. If your wife never closes her eyes anymore when you kiss her lips, that's not good. Okay, Yes, if you've watched Top Gun, you're on to me. I am referring to a song here, but it's the truth. When we begin to lose passion in our marriage, it slowly fades. I believe, just like in anything, **your marriage is either growing daily or dying gradually.** My hope is that we can create some passion and fire back into your marriage so that you will actually love being married again, or if you're single or even divorced, the next time you get married will be your last.

So many times, I will have men or couples that my wife and I will coach in their marriage and ask us what the key to marriage is. I have to say that there is no one key to unlocking and cracking the code for a great marriage. It truly is a combination. Most combinations, like the one we used on our lockers, have three numbers. So what I am going to share with you here are my three top principles for creating a marriage that will last a lifetime. I will share with you; some of Rachel and I's successes and, yes, our messes so that you can hopefully learn from our own mess-ups and not have to make the same mistakes yourself.

PRINCIPLE #1- THE POWER OF PRAYER

Trust me when I say **Prayer is not the least you can do; it is the most.** As I have grown as a husband over the years, I have also grown to understand the significance of prayer in my marriage. Here is a stat that really blew my mind when I first heard it. In the church, meaning people who identify themselves as Christians and who regularly attend church, there is a 50% divorce rate. That is crazy to me. So you would think that the divorce rate for people who don't go to church would be even higher, right? Well, actually, it's about the same. If you ask me why I think the number is the same, I would have to say it is because the enemy is all about destroying marriages, so if you are married and confessing to Christianity, you have a target on your back. We see marriages, people we know that we have gone to church with end up divorced, and it really hurts our hearts. So here is the stat that blew my mind and ever since has had me committed to praying daily with Rachel and for Rachel. There was a study done with over 1,000 married couples that, over a span of time, prayed daily as a couple. Each day, they set time in their schedules to come together and pray. At the end of this study, less than 1% of those couples were divorced. Think about that for a second. Less than 1%. That is amazing!

See, we know that we are going to have problems in our marriages. Most problems stem from major issues like money, sex, kids, and in-laws, and the major one is lack of communication. I am not going to go into crazy detail about these, but I can tell you we have personally experienced issues in our marriage because of all of the above. In my opinion, the real problem here is not the problem we are dealing with but the way we try to solve it. Too often, we seek advice from a specific friend, seek support from our parents, or even search the internet for a solution. While all along, the first thing we should be doing is praying to God.

GOD HAS A PHONE NUMBER

Another way to look at this would be to call upon God. This is why one of my favorite verses is Jeremiah 33:3. Think of it as **God's phone number! JER-E333!** Jeremiah 33:3 says, "Call to me, and I will answer you, and tell you great and unsearchable things." Like I said a second ago, many times, we will call a friend first to see what they think, ask how their spouse treats them, and then compare our situation to theirs, and so on. This is not right. The best thing we can do is to call upon God. He is the one with the wisdom that we want and need!

My pastor says prayer should be our first response, not our last resort. See, God created marriage. He is the creator of it. When you have a problem with something, normally the best course of action to get it fixed is to go back to the instruction manual, aka the Bible in this case, and if you had access to the creator of the product you needed help with, wouldn't it make sense to call that person directly? Of course, it does! So what I have learned over the 17 years of my marriage is that when there is an issue in my marriage, I need to immediately pray about it. I need to call upon God and ask for wisdom. In James 1:5, it says, "If any of you lacks wisdom, you should ask God, who gives generously to all without finding fault, and it will be given to you." That is good news to me! I don't know about you, but I feel that I need wisdom when it comes to my marriage every day. Actually, I need wisdom in every area of my life. I have known some people who will pray more for their favorite sports team to win than for their marriage to experience victory.

I am going to encourage you to commit to praying daily with your spouse. Men, I am going to ask you to take the lead here. God designed us to lead our marriages. So if the most powerful thing we can do for our marriage is to pray, then we have to be willing to get uncomfortable. I am going to give you the specific prayer that I like to say each day for my wife, and you can feel free to use it or parts of it. Here is what I pray for Rachel.

Heavenly Father, I pray that you will assist Rachel in becoming the Woman of God, wife, mother, and leader that you designed her to be. I pray for your Direction, Protection, and Correction, leading her with great wisdom each day. Thank you for giving her to me to Love, Honor, and Serve. Please help me love your daughter the way you want me to, and I ask for your blessing on our marriage. In Jesus' Name! Amen!

This is a simple prayer that literally takes 30 seconds or less each day to pray. Now, I'd like to encourage you to pause, re-read that prayer, cross out my wife's name, and replace it with the name of your husband or wife. You can change the wife to husband, mother to father, or love your daughter part of the prayer to love your son. The most important thing is that you take 30 seconds each day to say this prayer with an open heart to God. As you read through this prayer, think about what we are asking God to do here. I am asking God to really do what I can't. I am asking for his blessing upon my marriage. I am also asking him to help Rachel in multiple areas every day. I'm relinquishing control, which gives me peace of mind because I know He'll do the work that needs to be done. I also say this prayer for myself. Of course, I desire to be the Man of God, Husband, Father, and Leader God created me to be. Of course, I want God Directing, Protecting, and Correcting me daily. Of course, I want his wisdom daily to make the best decisions in my businesses, helping my clients, or most importantly, how I lead my family. **This prayer thing I take seriously. It is the secret to my success.** The thing about it is, God didn't make prayer a secret. He designed it as our way to communicate with him, ask for his advice, and to help us with things like our marriage.

I hope that this is helping you, my friend. This is why I have prayer as the first thing I do as a part of my Hour of Power. I don't believe there is a single thing more important or more powerful than this. I long for God's wisdom in my life. I also love to say thank you during this time for the blessings in my life!

PRAYING WITH YOUR SPOUSE

Okay, so now what about praying with your spouse? This is where I see a lot of men freak out. This can be intimidating if you have never done this before. Yes, it can be intimidating, but it can also be something that, if you're willing to do it, creates more intimacy in your marriage than anything else you can do. See, when we think of intimacy, most of us men think about physical intimacy. At least, that is what I always think of. Then our marriage coach one day told me, "Curt, there are actually three levels of intimacy." He said, "you, like most men, only think about the 3rd level of intimacy and go right to the sex part, but actually, there are two other levels. There is Spiritual Intimacy, and then the second level is Emotional Intimacy. With women, these matter way more than physical intimacy most of the time." A light-bulb moment for me, I must admit! "So what you're saying is that that could be one of the reasons why sex in my marriage isn't happening as often as I would like?" Bingo!

I will talk more about sex and Purity in Principle number 3. Just know that **praying with your spouse is a foundational principle to create more intimacy in your marriage.**

So the question I get many times is, "How do I pray with my spouse? It really is an easy answer. **You just do it!** I can tell you right now, especially to my brothers out there, that most of our wives are longing for this right now. Yes, you have to be vulnerable. You have to be willing to let her know you don't have a doctorate in prayer yet, and that you will probably fumble your words a little bit. Trust me, she doesn't care, and neither does God. It's your heart that matters most in this situation. The simple fact that you are stepping up and showing a desire to lead, the way God designed you to lead, is powerful. So my encouragement is to set aside 5–10 minutes a day to do a devotional together as a couple and start that devotional time with prayer. If you don't know what to pray, my encouragement to you would be to pray the same prayer over you and your wife as you pray in private to God. I don't think you can ask God too many times for these things, and remember to give him thanks at the same time for the blessing of your marriage.

Can I share with you what has happened in our marriage over the years since we created this as a foundation for our marriage? Our communication has gone through the roof. We rarely ever have fights, disagreements, or issues. I think one of the major reasons is that we have a set time each day to come together in prayer where we are being led with wisdom and are able to talk about difficult things like money, sex, kids, etc. These issues, when they are not talked about, many times create blow-ups in marriages. This is exactly what the enemy is trying to do. Most of the devotions that we do on different topics like sex, communication, kids, money, etc., always have questions that allow us to talk about things, which has been huge. If I could give you a couple of recommendations here, I would recommend anything that Jimmy and Karen Evans do. Their teachings have blessed our marriage in so many ways, and they lead the number one Marriage Ministry in the world called XO Marriage. So, friend, I'd like to encourage you today to make prayer your first response in your marriage rather than your last resort. I believe, with all my heart, that it will bless you more than you can ever think, hope, or imagine!

PRINCIPLE #2- THE POWER OF PRIORITY

This principle is a big one, especially in my marriage. I don't know how your spouse is, but it is very important to Rachel that she is number one. We have seen this principle be a blessing to people's marriages and also be a huge reason why there are so many problems in one's marriage. One of my favorite chapters in the Bible is Genesis Chapter 2. This is where the story of a woman is told. I love how God says in Genesis 2:18, "It is not good for man to be alone. I will make a suitable helper for Him." He then goes on to create the woman from the ribs he had taken from the man. The word says, in verse 23, "This is now bone of my bones and flesh of my flesh; she shall be called woman, for she was taken out of man." The next verse is huge. 24 "That is why a man leaves his father and mother and is united to his wife, and they become one flesh." **The truth is that when we get married, based on God's design, we become one with our spouse.** We are called to leave and cleave. In this verse, we are called to leave our mom or dad. That is why many ceremonial things in a wedding have the father giving away his daughter to her husband. He is now in charge of protecting and providing for her.

The reason I wanted to share this example of leave and cleave first is that, generally, this is one of the first issues of priority that couples will face in marriage. For me, I grew up a momma's boy. My mom and I were super close, so when Rachel and I first got married, I would take my mom's side on things, defend her, enable her, and so on, which would really upset Rachel. Why was Rachel so upset? Because she didn't feel number 1. I wasn't making her a priority. I see this happen a lot with guys who are really close to their moms, especially those of us who didn't grow up with a present father in the home. My mom always loved Rachel from day one, so I was lucky that I had a supportive mom who didn't speak negatively about my wife, as I have seen happen to other couples, which if that is happening in your marriage, I would highly encourage you to pray for wisdom about that and ask God for guidance there, as that can be very destructive when you have a parent who is in your ear, talking negatively about your husband or wife. Who you get wisdom from in your marriage is so important and, in my opinion, has a lot to do with whether a couple stays married or not. Rachel and I are still married today because we both had sound people in our lives that we have turned to for wisdom over the years. So, back to priority!

YOUR SPOUSE COMES FIRST!

I could go into a million scenarios here when it comes to making your Spouse a Priority, but I will just give you the 1 or 2 that tend to be the biggest problems and what we have experienced in our marriage. Early on in our marriage, it was easy to find time for each other. Then things get complicated fast. You buy your first house, which requires a lot of time and energy. You get that dream job you wanted with a salary that you think means you are going to work 40 hours a week for a high income, which actually means we are going to work way more than we think for less money, and because you have probably bought more house than you should have, that new car, and other stuff, you have to put in those hours. This happens pretty quickly in many situations. For me, early in our marriage, this is exactly what happened. We bought the house, got nice cars, and I worked late at least 2-3 nights a week until 8 pm. I feel like I'm missing something here. Oh yeah, KIDS! This is where it gets interesting. In my opinion, this is where the priorities really come into play.

Kids are precious bundles of joy that save you money on your taxes, but they can really mess up your intimacy in a marriage. Now please understand that I love our kids, and I'm sure you love yours too, but can we be real here? They add a whole other dynamic to being married. Once you have a child, it changes things. It is a 24/7 commitment that is going to require a lot of time, energy, and money. **One of the greatest wisdom nuggets Rachel and I have ever received in our marriage over the years is to put each other first.** Since early on in our marriage, we have always taken a trip each year, just her and I, without the kids. We make time for each other to put our marriage first and to do what healthy people do in healthy marriages. I have told you how we come together each morning for prayer and devotion. That is the foundation for our marriage. So what about at night? Right now, our two youngest are still at home. Having a 16-year-old daughter and a 17-year-old son at home can be awkward when it comes to having sex. So guess what we did? We told them, "Listen, kids, when the bedroom door is shut at night when we go to bed, stay away because yes, we are more than likely having sex." It was freeing to just own it instead of being weird about it, always wondering if the kids could hear us, etc. We have told them, listen, God designed sex for marriage, and when you get married, we don't want it to be awkward for you. So we chose the path to just be straight up with them. This is making each other a priority.

We also make time each week for a date night. Our schedules are both busy; there are always sports and other stuff but we are proactive about our date night. This is non-negotiable for us. When you first fell in love, most of us dated. Why does this stop when we get married and start having kids? So, date nights are a must! We have coached a lot of couples on marriage, and this is one of the first things we recommend. The kids will be fine with a sitter for a couple of hours. These are things that we must put in place to create a thriving marriage that will last a lifetime. If we don't make time for each other and let our jobs, kids, or stuff like TV, softball, or golf league, take the place of the most important thing in our life other than Jesus, which is our marriage, we are destined for some problems. When we make serving our spouse our number one priority, a beautiful marriage is the result we get! So here is your homework. Before moving on, take a second right now to ask your spouse or significant other what night works best for date night. Set this in stone: the day of the week, the time, and schedule it. Protect this time, prepare each week as needed, and commit to following through by taking time to invest in your marriage!

PRINCIPLE #3–THE PRINCIPLE OF PURITY!

Alright, I am going to go deep here on this topic, so I want to prepare you. This is something that I have prayed about, how much to say or not, and I believe that transparency is freedom. I have nothing to hide; there are no secrets in my life, and my mission is to help you create a Champion Life with this book.

So let me share with you why of all the things I could have chosen for the third principle, I chose Purity. I think it really goes back to the simple fact that God created marriage to be something beautiful. A man and a woman being together, we were told to be fruitful and multiply, he would bless the union, and so on. Here is the problem with that. Many of us haven't done Marriage the way God designed us to do. I have already addressed the lack of prayer and priority that I see in marriages today and I'm sure as you read through those, you could identify with a couple of things that may have even caused problems in your own marriage. So now I want to cover the

Purity part, because like I said this book is all about giving you Wisdom and Principles that have completely changed my life, marriage, business, etc. So when it comes to Purity, I can only tell you that I caused a lot of pain and issues in our marriage because of my lack of this Principle early on in our marriage.

Sex is designed for you and your spouse. That is God's design. The Bible talks a lot about sexual immorality. The book of Proverbs talks a lot about the adulterous woman and warns us men about her. I can only speak about what it's like from a man's perspective on this subject, but I can tell you that the desire for sex, in many men, is a constant. It is a dominating energy that consumes the mind, and for many men, I know and me, it must be a daily focus of asking God to give us the right focus. One of the first success books I ever read, Think and Grow Rich by Napoleon Hill, had a whole chapter titled The Power of Sex Transmutation that talked all about this. Paraphrasing the chapter, he basically said that when you can learn how to transfer your energy from thinking about sex all day long into business, you will be unstoppable. See, I have seen some very successful men who had amazing families, great businesses, and incredible lives lose it all because of the word "sex." They couldn't control the desire and appetite they had for it. They let their flesh control them, not the power of the Holy Spirit. Ultimately, because of their lack of self-control, they played with fire and got burnt. It is one of the reasons that my wedding band has the name Jesus on it. Every time I look at my ring, I not only think about Rachel, but I think about my commitment to Christ and my marriage. This is a level of protection that I have implemented into my life to protect the Purity of my marriage.

Now, before you think I'm some kind of saint or perfect husband, let me be honest. I didn't start out this way. From the very beginning, my marriage was basically built on a foundation of lust. As I said before, Rachel and I were two broken people that came together at the beginning of our relationship. I was a sex addict from day one, not knowing how to control those urges and not really knowing how to say NO. So when we got married, I had no idea about the importance of Purity and how that would truly affect every area of my life, not just my marriage. Getting married in Vegas was how it all started for us, and you know what they say. What happens in Vegas stays in Vegas. The only problem with that is that it is just a saying. The truth is, no matter what you do, it is going to have residual consequences that will affect your life, marriage, business, etc. At that point in our lives, our pre-Jesus days, we were all about the party life, having fun, etc. So on our second night of marriage as newlyweds, I decided and lobbied that we would get a friend to join us. It would be fun. That is where my mind went. Of course, Rachel has always wanted to make me happy, so she was in. So yes, we did what you probably shouldn't do in Vegas and hired a hooker to come to our room. This is not the best way to start off your marriage; trying to create the best Purity. This then went on to me being unfaithful in the early years of our marriage while I was traveling for work on the road. I even pulled her into my addiction, asking her to watch pornography, go to strip and sex clubs, and other things that pretty much destroyed the Purity of our marriage, along with trust, and created many other problems. These decisions, made early on in our marriage, caused years of hardship in our marriage. Rachel and I have been married for almost 17 years, and I can honestly say that this one area and my lack of understanding of its importance robbed us of well over a decade of Peace in Harmony in the areas of intimacy because of my lack of understanding of the importance of Purity.

GUARD YOUR INTIMACY

The truth is that God designed intimacy for you and your spouse. That is it! You have to guard this intimacy, my friend. We no longer let anything or anyone into this area of our lives except for Jesus. I used to think it was weird to pray about our sex life, but then I realized it was one of the biggest areas in my life that I needed help with. Now it is not awkward at all. If you're not praying to God and asking him for his help in this area, please do. I need his Direction, Protection, and Correction in this area as much or more than in any other area of my life. It is just the facts.

So let me share a couple of things that I have found to help Rachel and I take our marriage to the next level in this area and **Protect our Purity!**

1. My number one recommendation is to make sure you are having sex! This is so important for a healthy marriage. This is one of the biggest reasons for infidelity in a marriage. Ladies, you are the only person that can fulfill this duty for your husband, so please don't withhold. This took my wife a long time to understand and be obedient to. As you can imagine, she didn't always feel like doing it, but she doesn't live based on her feelings, but more on her commitments to being a godly wife and giving her husband her best. For many men, this is our main love language; once again, our wives are the only persons or things that should be fulfilling this area. Now, men, we must understand that we must also do our part here. Most of our wives are like crock pots, not microwaves. We can't just come home after a long day of work, and she has been taking

care of the kids, and just expect her to always be in the mood. We need to set the mood early in the day, lighten her load, help with the kids, and let her know how thankful we are and how grateful we are for her. Schedule her a massage every once in a while, take her on that weekly date night, etc. You know what I mean? The last thing I will say in this area is to look to serve her, not just get your own needs met.

2. The second thing I want to recommend to create a healthy marriage and sex life and protect the Purity of your marriage is to get rid of any baggage from the past or present in the form of sexual immorality. Men, if you are looking at any type of pornography, please stop! Studies show that over 64% of men struggle with pornography on a monthly basis, a stat that really blows my mind when it comes to women and couples. Over 50% of women say they watch pornography on a monthly basis, generally more soft porn, and that over 96% of women have watched porn with their partner and say it improves sex. Now, friends, these are some staggering numbers. This comes from a survey the Barna group did, which is a very reputable source. This doesn't surprise me because I was a part of those numbers for years. The enemy had me duped into thinking this was helpful for our marriage and sex life as well. The bottom line is marriage, and especially sex, was designed for you and your spouse only. Not for any other random person or a person on a phone you watch or even a mental picture in your mind. Jesus says in Matthew 6:27-28 You have heard it said, "You shall not commit adultery. 28 But I tell you that anyone who looks at a woman lustfully has already committed adultery with

her in his heart." The truth is, friends, that watching porn is really no different than committing the real act of adultery with another person. This, I believe, is why porn is so destructive and serves as a gateway to other things, such as marital affairs. It is something that I have overcome with the help of some close men and mentors, being open about it with my wife, and most importantly, daily prayer with God.

3. The last thing I want to recommend doing to help take your marriage and Purity to the next level is this. If there has been some past hurt, infidelity, or anything like that, you have to **let it go.** You can't continue to live with unforgiveness, lack of trust, or constantly bring up old stuff and expect to have a fulfilled marriage. I consider this a Purity issue because it really has a lot to do with your heart. When we are so consumed with living in the past, focused on what our partner has done to us, how they hurt us, and so on, it is going to be really hard to create a beautiful marriage filled with passion and intimacy. My wife could probably go deeper into detail, as I know this is something that she dealt with for years, to the point that it almost killed her. She had so much unforgiveness, bitterness, and resentment towards me that it caused her to get really sick with stomach issues. There is a saying **that unforgiveness is like drinking poison and expecting the other person to die.** The only person that it is killing inside is you. Our unforgiveness doesn't affect the other person; It infects us. So if you truly want a marriage that is filled with passion and intimacy and it's important to you to Protect your Purity, this is a must to make this happen.

GET A MARRIAGE COACH

You may need a professional coach to work through some past hurts, and that's okay. Rachel and I have had a coach our entire 17 years. I can confidently say that we would not be married today if it weren't for this coach. John Jung was and still is a mighty blessing to our marriage! Trust me when I say that you can do it. Trust can be re-established, and a new level of love for your spouse can be obtained! I have seen it happen in our marriage! The last thing I will say, as you're working through this, is to get a new vision for your marriage. The past is the past, so leave it there. Learn from it, allow it to make you stronger, but focus on creating a new vision for your marriage. I firmly believe that if you commit to doing marriage God's way, you will have the marriage you desire. I am going to leave you with a couple verses from Ephesians that I turn to often to remind me of God's design for marriage. I would encourage you to study these verses often and ask God for wisdom on how you can apply them to your marriage, along with the other things I have talked about so far in this section. When you begin to implement the things I have talked about here, things will change for you, or if things are good already, they will get even better!

Ephesians 5 21-33

"[21] Submit to one another out of reverence for Christ.

[22] Wives, submit yourselves to your own husbands as you do to the Lord. [23]. For the husband is the head of the wife as Christ is the head of the church, his body, of which he is the Savior. [24] Now, as the church submits to Christ, so also wives should submit to their husbands in everything.

²⁵ Husbands, love your wives, just as Christ loved the church and gave himself up for her

²⁶ to make her holy, cleansing[a] her by the washing with water through the word,

²⁷ and to present her to himself as a radiant church, without stain or wrinkle or any other blemish, but holy and blameless.

²⁸ In this same way, husbands ought to love their wives as their own bodies. He who loves his wife loves himself.

²⁹ After all, no one ever hated their own body, but they fed and cared for their body, just as Christ does the church—

³⁰ for we are members of his body.

³¹ For this reason, a man will leave his father and mother and be united to his wife, and the two will become one flesh.

[b] ³² This is a profound mystery—but I am talking about Christ and the church. ³³ However, each one of you also must love his wife as he loves himself, and the wife must respect her husband."

CHAPTER 10

RAISING CHAMPION ADULTS

I remember a teaching I heard one day from one of my mentors, Tim Goad, that has truly stuck with me over the years. It was all about Generational Leadership. It involved thinking about everything we do and how it will affect the 3rd generation. So another words: not just our kids, but their kids. Proverbs 13:22 says, "A good person leaves an inheritance for their children's children." Now, Solomon is talking about financial wealth here. However, I like to think of that inheritance as more than financial. I believe this is deeper than just finances, although that is important. I believe the wisdom that we help our kids learn through teaching them many of the fundamentals I have discussed in this book is more valuable than money. In the next chapter, we will talk a lot more about money, but first, I want to end this section by talking about how we can not just focus on raising good kids but, more importantly, future Champion Adults.

I will be honest with you; this has been one of the most difficult things for me to learn over the years. How to be a Loving, Encouraging, and Empowering Father and Leader for my children. Leadership in the home is so crucial. There are so many studies that show that when the home lacks a male leader, the children are far more likely to end up in trouble, struggle in many ways, etc. Here is a pretty staggering statistic I will share with you regarding salvation. This is for us men. **When the husband gives his life to Christ, over 93% of his family gets saved. If the wife gets saved first, it's only 17%, and if it's the kids first, it's only 3.5%.** Those are some pretty incredible numbers, and you can see why I have such a passion for helping married men know Jesus! It truly has a massive impact!

As I have said before, I didn't grow up with a godly leader in the home, so this has been a constant mission for me to search and learn. Certain things like fitness and business have become much easier for me. This parenting thing, I must admit, has been hard! In our early years of marriage, when the kids were young, I was such a train wreck that I knew there was some damage done. Kids, when they are young, are so moldable. This is why you can teach a young kid 2 or 3 multiple languages way easier than you can teach somebody who is 40 like me. So what we teach our kids, their environment from the early stages, and how we speak life into them truly matters way more than we realize. I am not an expert in this area, so I don't plan on giving you my top 10 ways to be a great parent. I'm sure there are plenty of better teachers for this, and books you can read. All I want to do is share what lessons I have learned in my journey, probably more of what not to do, and a couple of stories that maybe you can relate to. Here are a few lessons I have learned in my 17 years as a dad!

KIDS SPELL LOVE T-I-M-E

The first and most important thing that I can tell you and encourage you to do is to just spend time with your kids. Kids spell LOVE, TIME! No matter what the age, TIME is flying by, and before you know it, your kids will be grown up and gone, and you will be wondering where that time went. As my two youngest are already 17 and 16, I sometimes find myself thinking, "I wish I had done this or that." Friend, I don't want you to have any regrets, and I want you to learn from my mistakes. One of the things that I wish I had done earlier on was to be more present. As I have mentioned before, you can be somewhere physically but not mentally. Now, I do believe I have been a great dad. My wife has told me that many times and one of the things I am grateful for is the amount of time that I have had with my kids. I chose to be an entrepreneur early on for that one reason so that I could be in control of my time. That decision allowed me to work from home while my kids were growing up, from 3 to pretty much now. So I am here every day to see them off to school, and all the way through high school, to be here when they get home from the bus. So I do have so many magic moments. However, I can also remember being there, saying how cool it was, and spending time with them physically, but not mentally.

I can remember playing baseball in the backyard, pitching batting practice to Carson, yet while I was doing that, I was thinking about the calls I needed to make, what deals I needed to close, and so on. So my point of sharing this with you is one thing. **When you spend time with your kids, be fully present!** I once heard somebody say that your kids don't want your presents, they want your PRESENCE. That really stuck with me. Now, if your kids are anything like mine, they want both, but that's another story. So my encouragement to you would be to schedule a date day or specific time each week to spend with each one of your children one-on-one. Lock in that hour on your calendar just like you would an important business meeting or your date night with your wife, and spend that hour connecting with your kid, being fully present. Then, once or twice a year, spend the whole day with them. Go do something fun and really connect. My 16-year-old daughter Carli and I just had a Daddy/Daughter Day a couple of weeks ago, where we flew to New York City for the day. We got up early to catch a 6 a.m. direct flight to New York City and had a blast. We went to Times Square, ice skated at the Rockefeller Center, visited the 9/11 site, had a couple of slices of New York Style pizza, shopped at all kinds of stores, got her that taxi ride she wanted, and just had fun. I can tell you I slept well that night after the 20,000 steps we got in that day. It was an incredible day, something that she wanted to do, and I am glad I was able to make it possible. Now, it doesn't have to be that extreme. You don't have to spend a bunch of money or whatever. It is a once-a-year deal. The other days are for just having lunch, grabbing a cup of coffee, going on a walk, shopping at Walmart, as that is where she likes to go, or whatever. As for my son, he just loves to throw baseballs, watch sports together, golf, and so on. It's just about being proactive and building in those margins to spend time with your kids and let them know that they are more important than your job, boss, or business even. This takes focus and intention, but the investment pays big returns and is generational.

SPEAKING LIFE–THE LOOKING GLASS THEORY

Proverbs 18:21 says, "The tongue has the power of life and death, and those who love it will eat its fruit." I am convinced that the words we speak over our children shape them more than we realize. I remember when a mentor of mine told me to start paying attention to how other people talk about their kids. He said I would start to notice certain parents call their kids names like Champion, Stud, Princess, etc. Then other parents would call their kids little devils, terrorists, and stubborn. Maybe you have experienced this in your own childhood where you had the experience of being called things like that or being told that you weren't ever going to amount to anything; you were lazy; you weren't any good; you were the reason your family was broke; and so on. I believe this kind of crap becomes generational. You see, it passes down from generation to generation. This is why I mentioned the 3rd generation philosophy earlier because for things to change, we have to change first. I know for me, I had to be the one that said no more. I am drawing a line in the sand. I am creating a new legacy for the Tucker family line. There are certain things I am no longer going to stand for.

So the second thing that I think is so important in building Champion Adults is how we speak over our kids. I said earlier that we are the CEO's. The Chief Encouragement Officers! How we talk to them, encourage them, and empower them matters. This makes me think of what is called the Looking Glass theory, which basically says that we become what we believe other people think most about us. We see our reflection of who we are like a mirror, in what the most important people in our lives think about us. So, if we are constantly building our kids up, telling them how much of a Champion they are and what we are proud of about them, this is preparing them to be that Champion in a major way. This really goes along with the Law of the Thermostat that I was talking about earlier. We become the average of the five people we hang out with the most. They are the ones influencing us, speaking into our lives, and so on. So for our kids, if we are the most dominant influencers in their lives, you can see the importance of this. So speaking life into our kids regardless of their age, being that consistent voice of encouragement, in my opinion, is one of the best things we can do as parents to help build our kids into the Champions that God created them to be.

ALWAYS REMEMBER THEY WERE GOD'S KIDS FIRST

The third and last thing I want to share with you that I hope will give you peace is this. Always remember that before your kids were yours, they belonged to God. Actually, they still do belong to Him. We have just been given the opportunity here on earth to champion them. To Love, Encourage, and Empower them to be the Champion Leaders that God created them to be. It is one of the most important stewardship opportunities we will ever be given. The major reason I wanted to share this perspective with you of our kids being God's kids first, though, is that it brings me great peace. I don't know about you, but I can be a worrier at times. The enemy is the king of lies, and I believe from the moment our kids are born, the worry begins. If you have ever lost your kid at a retail store for 5 minutes, you know exactly what I'm talking about. Panic can set in quickly. Today, as my kids are older, I find myself wanting to protect them even more than when they were little. I can worry about them driving home from practice at night. Sometimes we go to bed at 9, and they are not home yet.

What I have learned that gives me peace is to just remind myself that they belong to God. I just pray for his Direction and Protection over them, and I feel an instant Peace. Once again, prayer is not the least we can do; it's the most. I pray for my kids daily and every morning with them before they walk out the door for school. This is by design, by the way. It is one of the highlights of my day. I also believe that I am showing them what it looks like to be a parent who cares in hopes that they will establish the same rituals when they have kids. This is the 3rd generation mindset!

You are creating a legacy, my friend, and it begins with your children. As I get older, I sometimes visualize a picture of Rachel and I on a wall at a beach house. That beach house is the house that we worked hard to earn and to have in the family for many years to come. That house is filled with our kids, grandkids, and great-grandkids. I visualize seeing and hearing the conversations taking place about how amazing Rachel and I were, the sacrifices we made, and the life example we lived. We got to enjoy many years with them all in this beach house, but at this point, we are no longer there physically, but our legacy lives on with them. So the truth is that we will all die someday, but our legacy will live on. It will live on with our kids, grandkids, and the generations after that. The way I love, pray, and lead my kids today sets my legacy up to be the kind of legacy I believe I will be proud of. So, no matter how old your children are, it is never too late to start thinking about your legacy and spending time with them. Pray for them daily, Be present if you can if they're still at home, and let them know how much you love them and how amazing you think they are. Your legacy is in the making!

CHAPTER 11

CREATING THE RIGHT MONEY MINDSET

Money is meaningless! That doesn't seem like a good way to start off a chapter on creating the right money mindset, does it? What I mean is that money will be meaningless if it is the only thing that you focus on. In this section of the book, and particularly in this chapter, I am going to help you develop the right money mindset that will set you up to have more abundance in your life. I believe that many of us have poor mindsets when it comes to money, and therefore, because of that, we don't attract it to us like a magnet; we actually put up this invisible forcefield that keeps it far away from ever coming into our hands. So in this section, I am going to cover the things that I have done in my life and my experience going from being broke, busted, and disgusted when it comes to finances to having more today in my life than I ever thought was possible.

As I lay these truths out, all I can encourage you to do is Believe! Believe that the same can happen for you! If you are already doing well in this area of life, then I will guess that you are already doing many of the things that I am going to talk about. The reason why I am confident in that is that I didn't make all this stuff up. What I am going to share with you is just information that I have gathered over the last 20 years of persistent searching for wisdom and knowledge on creating financial wealth for my family that will last for generations and me, and more importantly, for me, is Eternal. So yes, I am definitely going to quote the Bible a few times, as the truth is Jesus talked about money, and I believe the Bible is filled with great and sound financial advice. It has certainly been a major contributor to developing my Money Mindset over the years.

Developing the Right Money Mindset is very much like the examples of creating a Champion mindset earlier in the book when it comes to treating the mind like a garden. You must do the work of getting rid of all the weeds and root systems that are not serving you anymore if you want to develop a garden that is actually able to grow and sustain. I find that this is just as true when it comes to money. So before I go deep into the steps of creating more money in your life, let me share with you just a few things I believe hold people back.

IS MONEY THE ROOT OF ALL EVIL?

Here is a big one that my momma used to tell me all the time to watch out for, and I see other people using it a lot. She would say, "you gotta be careful because the Bible says money is the root of all evil. Actually, that is not what the Bible says. The Bible says in 1 Timothy 6:10, "For the love of money is the root of all kinds of evil. Some people, eager for money, have wandered from the faith and pierced themselves with many griefs. "The key word here to FOCUS on is the love of money. Jesus said something similar in his teachings found in Matthew 6:24-25, where he said, "No one can serve two masters. Either you will hate the one and love the other, or you will be devoted to the one and despise the other. You cannot serve God and money. Do you see what is going on here? Money is not the problem; it's the way we look at money. If we begin to love money more than we love Jesus, we have a problem. If we begin to think that money can take the place of Jesus and fill the void in our hearts, we have a problem. If we begin to wander from our faith and begin to focus more on money than on Jesus, that is where we have some major problems. This is why Jesus is saying you will be devoted to one and despise the other. He then says, "You cannot serve God and money."

YOU CAN SERVE GOD WITH MONEY

So what I believe to be true here, friends is... money isn't the root of all evil; the love of money is, and when we put that as the first focus above, Jesus, we have a problem. However, I believe If we create the right money mindset and commit ourselves to use the resources that we are blessed with to build the Kingdom first, then I believe that we can serve God with money. I love the quote If He can get it through you, He will get it to you. Think about that for a second. Re-read that quote again and let that sink in. **If He can get it through you, He will get it to you!** Money is definitely needed in our society today. It is pretty much as important as oxygen these days. If you don't have enough money to pay for your mortgage on your home, buy groceries at the store, or put gas in your car, you are going to have a problem. Praying that God will magically show up and put the gas you need in your car is probably not going to happen. What is more likely is that He will bless you with the money from the work you put in to pay for the gas. So my point is that we must get the right perspective on money, that it's not the root of all evil. Money, in my opinion, is neutral.

There are plenty of bad people that have a lot of money that they have gotten by lying, cheating, and stealing. There are also a lot of good people that have accumulated a lot of money by providing a product or service that creates value in somebody's life or business and solves a problem. We are going to talk more about this in the next chapter. What I want you to consider and get your mind around is that money is a blessing! When you ask God to help you earn more of it, and you have a plan to be a good steward of it, I believe wholeheartedly that is the beginning of your creating Financial Freedom in your life. That is exactly what has happened to me.

MONEY CAN BE A BLESSING FOR MANY GOOD THINGS

Think about this. As I said before, IF GOD CAN GET IT THROUGH YOU, HE WILL GET IT TO YOU. How are these examples below funded?

1. Your Church, Your Pastor, The Staff, The Utilities, The Ministries they support, The food pantry, and everything else that is going on at that church. All this is funded by people who are giving their Tithes and Offerings to the church. Without people having money to give, this church can't exist. As a matter of fact, Josh Tolley, in his book that I would highly recommend, named Evangelpreneur, talks a lot about wealth and hits on the fact that many churches each year close their doors for lack of finances.

2. Providing Clean Water in Poor Countries Like Ethiopia and Uganda: One of the things that I am passionate about is providing clean water in areas

where innocent children die every day from diseases. These young children and their mothers have to travel miles each day to get clean water for basic needs like bathing, cooking, and dishes. Every day, they risk being attacked by wild animals, being kidnapped, raped, and having their children trafficked for sex. This is happening every day, and when you help fund a water yard in a country like this, you give that mom and her kid's access to clean water right in their local village.

3. Struggling single moms or widows- Have you ever seen a single mom busting her tail working three jobs, trying to figure out how she is going to get her kids to the functions she needs, the emotional burden she is probably dealing with inside because she can't be at her kids' games, the fear of how the light bill is going to be paid, or how school supplies, shoes, and fees will be paid? Or maybe the widow who was left behind with not much, and that is why she is the greeter at Walmart.

I have just given you three examples, with some details for people that are in need. I could go on and on with examples like sex trafficking, missionaries, organizations for kids, inner city programs, etc. There are so many things that, at the end of the day, take money to fund, support, and make sure the mission gets carried out. Without financial resources, nothing happens. I haven't talked much about your basic needs like Housing, Transportation, Food, Insurance, Utilities, and so on. So can we all agree now that we need money to survive? So, once we realize that money is not evil, that we need it, and that with it, we can absolutely enhance our lifestyle and bless a lot of other people and organizations, I believe we can start to create some

Financial Freedom in our lives. Freedom many times starts in our minds. Okay, so let's dive into how you are going to create Financial Freedom for you and your family!

CREATE A CLEAR VISION

Step 1- Get a vision of where you want to be financially and why it's important to you.

Vision, Vision, Vision! If you were to hang around me on a daily basis, you would hear me say this word a lot. The simple reason is that **you have to know where you're going if you want to get there.** In your health, in your marriage, and YES, in your finances as well. Once you know what you want and why you want it, we can figure out how! A GPS on your phone is only as good as the directions that you put into it. So if you haven't established where you're trying to go, it's not going to be of much help. So I can tell you when I ended up broke and bankrupt in my mid 20's, I started to realize I needed to make some changes. I needed to develop a New Vision, create a new relationship with money, and get as much wisdom as I could from other people who were living the life that I wanted to live.

So one of the first things that I did was develop the New Vision. That number for me was $10,000 a month. For my family and me at that time, when we were pretty much broke, that number seemed so amazing and life-changing, and even though it was a lot at the time, I felt it could be attainable. After I wrote that number down, I then started to write down why it was important to me. Why was it so important that I figure out how to earn that amount of money? At the time, I wasn't an entrepreneur; I was actually working in the car business, and because of my mindset, I was struggling. When you bankrupt your family, trust me, it can get you down in many ways. I share this with you with full transparency because I want you to know that if you are there right now, Financial Freedom in your life is 100% possible. I also want to help you in this section get rid of any excuses or, as I like to say, the story that you have been telling yourself that has basically kept you broke. I see too many people living broke because of the sob story they tell themselves every day. They don't have the skills, they have never been taught about money, they have debt, they don't make enough money, they got fired from their job, and so on. None of that matters.

You can start today by creating a New Vision. Leave the old stories and excuses behind you, and get going towards creating a life of Financial Freedom that will allow you to have fun in life. So when I set this goal to earn $10,000 a month, I wrote down all the reasons why and what I was going to do with the money. One of the greatest quotes I have ever heard about money and creating wealth is this. It is so important to **GIVE EVERY DOLLAR A JOB!** Meaning, when you get money, make sure that you know where it is going ahead of time. This keeps you from just spending it on aimless things. I will go deeper into this principle of paying yourself first here shortly. So I knew when I started to earn that 10,000 dollars a month what I was going to do with that money. So now the reality is I was only earning $2,000 a month when I made these decisions to focus on $10,000, so if that is where you're at, it's okay. For illustration purposes, I am going to use $10,000 a month as an example in this book a lot to help make this practical for you. If you already earn that or more, then you can go to $100,000 a month as your example, or even a million a month. If you are at that level, you are way above me, so feel free to reach out to me and give me some money tips!

So as you begin to start creating this New Money Mindset and dreaming bigger than ever before, I will tell you; it's natural to have some doubt, negative thoughts, etc. That is why I am talking about mindset, aka Your Direction of Focus, as creating wealth really begins here. I had to fill my mind with thoughts, images, and Bible verses to meditate on in the very beginning. Here are a couple of verses that I locked on to very early that helped me get this mindset right. I will tell you that I read these over and over daily, meditated on them as if they were 100% absolute truth, and got into an agreement with God. Philippians 4:19 says, "And my God will meet all your needs according to the riches of his glory in Christ Jesus." So when I would fear, worry, and doubt about being broke again or our current situation, I would say this over and over. I knew 100% that God was going to meet all my needs. Now that I knew my needs would be met, as most of our basic needs are met if you live in America especially, I could move on to my wants. I wanted to have financial abundance in my life so I could provide a certain lifestyle for my family, as well as support my church, build water yards and support single moms that were struggling. I could not do that at $2,000 a month. I couldn't even support my own family, let alone help anybody else. Now before I tell you the next verse, let me share a quick story that absolutely changed my life and the first thing I am going to recommend you do with your money.

IT'S NOT A DEBT YOU OWE, BUT A SEED THAT YOU SOW

Alright, if I lose you here, which is possible, I want you to take a deep breath and come back to me with an open mind. What I am about to share with you was one of the hardest things for me to do in my life in the very beginning. I was absolutely desperate, though, and I felt like, what did I have to lose when I said "Yes" to this? I am talking about my financial conversion and committing to tithing. If you're not familiar with what tithing is, it simply means taking 10% of your income, whatever you make from your job, earning from your business after expenses, what you bring home, and giving it to the church that you go to. This message in the Bible is probably the most disliked message of all and the one that people want to gloss over and not want to take to heart. We love the message of salvation, God's abundant grace, and that we can do all things through Christ. However, when the preacher starts preaching about giving 10% of our money to the church, we check out. Maybe I am just talking about myself here for the first 3 or 4 years of my going to church. I was cool with throwing a $10 or $20 bill in the offering plate here and there, but giving 10% of my income consistently was crazy.

Then, as I told you earlier in the book, we lost everything. House foreclosed, cars repossessed, marriage hanging on by a thread, and feeling broken in every way, especially financially. When you are financially broke, having to accept a car from a friend, government food assistance to feed your family, and people helping to pay for things like utilities, you can feel pretty low. **I know 100% that God brought me to that low point to get me to trust in Him fully and to make me realize that I needed help.** He will do that to us from time to time, and I look back today so happy and grateful that He did that to me.

So one evening, I came home from work, and Rachel met me in the kitchen. She said, "Curt, we need to start tithing. This is a conversation that we had talked about numerous times, but I would immediately get defensive, say there was no way that was possible, and change the subject. Now, God had been working on me for a while, and this time, I was open to the conversation. At this point, I was getting into God's word more, seeking wisdom and truth, and had actually been pondering over a set of verses around this subject. I want to share with you this passage of scripture and hopefully break it down for you in a way that will give you a whole new perspective on this subject and help you take this leap of faith that I took. If you open your heart and your Hand, God can and will bless you more than you ever thought, hoped, or imagined.

Malachi 6-12 says **6** "I, the Lord, do not change. So you, the descendants of Jacob, are not destroyed. **7** Ever since the time of your ancestors you have turned away from my decrees and have not kept them. Return to me, and I will return to you," says the Lord Almighty." But you ask, 'How are we to return?' **8** "Will a mere mortal rob God? Yet you rob me. "But you ask, 'How are we robbing you?'

"In tithes and offerings. **9** You are under a curse—your whole nation—because you are robbing me. **10** Bring the whole Tithe into the storehouse so that there may be food in my house. Test me in this," says the Lord Almighty, "and see if I will not throw open the floodgates of heaven and pour out so much blessing that there will not be room enough to store it. **11** I will prevent pests from devouring your crops, and the vines in your fields will not drop their fruit before it is ripe, "says the Lord Almighty. **12** "Then all the nations will call you blessed, for yours will be a delightful land," says the Lord Almighty.

Okay, so I am going to be completely transparent with you here. This is some challenging scripture. That doesn't once again discount the truth of it. How many of us, at some point, have turned away from God, especially in our finances? We say things like, "If I just get this raise, I will start to give. When

I get that promotion, we will be doing better, and I will give more. These verses scared me a little at first because I did not like the feeling of thinking that I was robbing God. In 2008, in my current situation, when I read this scripture and really chewed on it, discerning it and asking God for wisdom, I really felt like I was under a curse. I am just being completely honest. It was the darkest financial time of my life. I could feel God asking me to trust him in this area. I needed to release this to him. As I read verses 10–12, things really began to make sense to me. What I am about to tell you was a game changer for me, and I hope it is for you.

GOD DOESN'T NEED OUR MONEY

The truth is God doesn't need my money or your money. He is the owner of it all. It is really just a trust thing, and if he can trust you with a little, He will trust you with a lot. As I read the verses, I began to realize that **my Tithe wasn't a debt that I owed but a seed that I sowed.** When I gave 10% of my income as a way of saying thank you to God for the financial blessing in my life, God was taking that seed and using it to bless so many people, and in the process, it was blessing my family more and more. I read the scripture, and I started to see all the promises God was making when we were obedient to this principle. He says he will throw open the floodgates of heaven and pour out so much blessing on you and me that there won't be enough room to store it. Who doesn't want that? Then, as I continued reading, it says, "He will keep pests from devouring crops and fruit from falling before it is ripe," which basically means He will protect you and your financial resources. As a business owner, I think about all the times God has protected me from bad decisions, people and situations that have tried to come against me or my businesses, and things that were maybe meant for harm that turned out for my good. Wow, who doesn't want God's direction and protection over your businesses? Then it goes on to say, "Then all the nations will call you blessed, for yours will be a delightful land." As I read this, I could picture people looking at my family and me and saying, "Man, they are doing something right. They are so blessed! They live in a beautiful home, drive nice cars, take nice vacations, and have such an incredible life. That was what I pictured as I read this scripture and began to believe what was possible.

Can I tell you something, my friend? What I just described is the life that I live today! I wake up every day and thank God for the life I have. It truly is everything that is in these scriptures. He has blessed me with overflowing status in so many ways. He has protected me, my family, and my businesses, and yes, many people do call us BLESSED! For over a decade now, we have been committed to tithing and giving offerings on top of that to organizations like World Vision, where we have sponsored two children named Sharon and Shafi. This year we were actually able to fund our first water yard in Uganda with the help of some close friends and family. I am able to walk around with a couple of hundred dollar bills in my pocket at all times, ready and willing to bless a single mom with a big tip or just give because God puts it on my heart to give. I could tell you stories after stories of opportunities that I have had. Many of them I have forgotten, but I believe that person still remembers, and I know God knows. Generosity is now a huge driving force for me, something that pushes me every day to keep showing up and being my best, as I know that the financial resources that I am blessed with can and will be a huge blessing to others. So friends, all I can tell you is I am so thankful that my wife continued to encourage me all those times to Tithe and that our church kept asking us to trust in God in the areas of our finances. Some churches shy away from this, but our church doesn't. So if this has been a struggle for you, and you're not seeing the fruit you would like in the areas of your finances, this could be the one last thing you need to commit to. All I can say is Trust in God, Give generously with a grateful heart, and expect God to bless you and your family. That is his Promise!

CAN YOU BE TRUSTED

Wait, there is more! Here is what I mean. It is one thing to be generous with the wealth that we have, but we also must be trusted. The Bible says that those who can be trusted with a little can be trusted with a lot, right? That is good news if you are generous and also a good steward. See, it is one thing to give 10% back to the Lord in the form of the Tithe, but what about the other 90%? Yes, what you do with that absolutely matters. Now I feel like I need to tell you something before I go on any further. I truly want to help you become Financially Free, and I am going to share with you some strategies and tactics on not only how to create wealth but also how to grow it. However, first I just feel a stirring in my heart right now to talk about Stewardship.

See, I have been so blessed in the area of finances, and I believe it has been because of my commitment to doing things right. Now I'm not going to go crazy on certain subjects like good debt vs. bad debt, as there is such a thing; as how you should invest, whether you go all in on real estate vs. stocks, and that type of stuff. I will touch base on it. All of those things are definitely a part of being wealthy financially, and you can find a million books on that stuff. For me, I feel more called to talk to you about creating the right money mindset, having a heart of generosity, and the power of being a good steward. I do believe that **money just makes you more of who you are.** So some people's money just magnifies their selfishness, dysfunction, and so on, whereas money in the hands of the right people gets invested and multiplied for the Kingdom and generations to come. This is where the other 90% comes in.

So if we are making $10,000 a month and are committed to tithing 10% of our income, or $1000 a month, then where does the other $9,000 go? Well, that really depends on many variables. Are you a w-2 employee where you probably get taxed the most versus your income coming from your business, or maybe you started a side business and got a 1099? This is very important because there are a million tax advantages to being a 1099 or owning a business. By writing things off, you have the ability to significantly reduce your tax liability. Just being able to write off minor things like your cell phone, car, internet bill, part of your home if you work from home, meals that are related to a business conversation, trips, and so much more can really add up. At the end of the year, trust me, this can add up to a significant amount, which can save you thousands on taxes. The only thing I can tell you is to please find a good accountant. This is not an area to go cheap on. My accountant, whom I know 100%, has saved me thousands of dollars over the years, easily six figures. This is being a good steward and also taking advantage of the tax laws that are available when you have a business.

ALWAYS PAY YOURSELF FIRST

So while I'm talking about being a good steward of the 90%, this leads me to one of the most important things I believe you can do when it comes to creating financial freedom in your life, which is **PAY YOURSELF FIRST!** You will have to pay some taxes, but before you go pay everybody else, I encourage you to pay yourself first. Here is what I mean. Most people, when they get paid, immediately begin to pay bills. You know, they make the mortgage payment, then the car payment, the insurance, the grocery gets some of your money, your cell phone provider, utilities, maybe you go out to dinner and a movie. All of a sudden, boom, you're broke again. I hope not, but this is what I remember from my experience of being broke. I would be like, "Where did the money go? I gave it to everybody else. "Most people think I just need to make more money and I won't have this problem. That just isn't true. The more money you make, the more your lifestyle will increase. I have seen this happen to myself and countless people that I know. So, if all you do is make more money, you will just spend it on a nicer house, car, or better restaurant. By the way, I have nothing against any of those things. I live in a house four times the size of the house I lived in 13 years ago when I went bankrupt. My wife drives a Range Rover, and I love a good steak at a nice restaurant on date night!

The point I am trying to make here is that you first must make a decision backed by action that you will set aside a portion of your income and pay yourself first before you give all your money away to everyone else. That is how, over time, you will begin to create wealth. You won't be racking up debt, paying negative interest every month on credit cards, and feeling broke. Instead, you will have money in the bank, your wealth accounts will be growing with interest, and you will feel good about your sense of Stewardship. So here is what you have to commit to doing. When you get paid, just make a predetermined decision to pay yourself a percentage of your income. Ideally, I would recommend Tithe 10%, Saving 10%, and Investing another 10% minimum into something that will grow. Then pay all the bills. Now, I could really get off on a tangent here, but people do ask me this question all the time. They say, "Curt, I understand that I should save some money in case I get a flat tire, the dryer breaks, or maybe I want to take the family on vacation." That makes perfect sense. However, when it comes to investing, what should I invest in? That is a great question, and it really depends. What I mean is that it really depends on what is most important to you, what stage of life you're in, and what your risk tolerance is. All I can personally do is tell you what I have done over the years that has gotten me the greatest return when it comes to investing.

THE BEST INVESTMENTS!

Invest In You First—In my opinion, if you only have $100 to invest each month, you should invest that in yourself. I know I am giving an example of $10,000 a month with these numbers, but I understand there are a lot of people that don't come close to even that amount on a monthly basis. So if that is you, like it was for me, I would invest in you. Buy some books on business, leadership, or a particular business you would like to start. Invest in a course that can teach you a skill or two that you need to double your income, go to a conference, or even hire a coach. The thing I like about investing in myself is that nobody can ever take that from me. I have personally invested well over six figures in coaching, seminars, courses, books, and so on. I am 100% certain I would not be where

I am today in my life, marriage, and business without setting this as a foundational principle early on. So I believe that **the first thing you should invest in is YOU!** It will give you the greatest ROI on your time and money.

Invest in Your Business-Your business is what pays you. This is the cash machine that allows you to continue to make money. You want to make sure that you are always investing back into it. This will allow the business to grow, become more stable over time, and hopefully free you up to do other things. If you take all the money out of the business, you won't have a business anymore. So invest in your Brand, Systems, and Team that allows your business to operate. Invest more in marketing if you need more customers; invest in better systems if you feel your business could be more efficient, and invest in new team members if you feel overwhelmed and like you're doing everything. To Grow and Scale your business, you can't do it by yourself. Once again, find a coach or someone who has already done what you want to do, and make the investment!

Infinite Banking Account-This for me, would be an investment account in the form of a whole life insurance policy that operates more like an investment account. Someday you are going to want to retire, leave money to your children, and I'm sure many other things. Most of us have been trained to just put money into our 401 K's or the stock market. I think getting a good company match is a great idea, and contributing to your 401K is wise. However, I am an entrepreneur, and I want to best utilize my money NOW! I also understand that someday I am also going to have to pay taxes on the growth of my money that is in those types of accounts. So, with a properly set up Whole Life Insurance Policy, you can get all the benefits of investing with no risk, tax-free growth, and the benefit of a death benefit if something happens to you. These are all great, but there is one big major reason why I am a huge advocate for this being one of the first things you should start investing in. It's because it allows you to start creating your own bank. I like to call mine "The Tucker Family Bank." I would highly recommend my friend and wealth advisor, Matt Warren of Duvall Financial Group. Actually, I asked him to share real quickly what he thought were the major benefits, and here is what he had to say. 📖 A friend I greatly respect is completing a book. He's a believer in private family banking and asked me to write a couple paragraphs about it, to include in the financial section. Here it is…

IF YOU'RE LEGACY MINDED, WHOLE LIFE IS FOR YOU

With investing, knowns are our friend, and unknowns are our enemy. Incorporating the Infinite Banking Concept (IBC) into your financial foundation with properly structured whole life insurance gives you important certainties on several fronts:

- ✔ Control and access to your cash
- ✔ Guaranteed growth
- ✔ Tax-free access of that growth
- ✔ Guaranteed tax-free death benefit when you "graduate" from this life
- ✔ Whole life gives you guarantees that IUL's and variable life policies do not

Powerful forces such as the government, Wall Street, and financial planners have a vested interest in you NOT investing in permanent insurance–they'll tell you to "buy term and invest the difference." There are lots of holes in that plan. When the term ends, it's certain that when you die, there will be no death benefit. And, IF your investments grow (no certainty there), they'll be taxed at what the government decides they need from you later on.

Families that perpetuate generational wealth have a legacy mindset. They keep their capital within their control and compound it. Most incorporate IBC, so they or their heirs are independent of banks, Wall Street crashes, and taxation. We want to model what has been proven over generations, which is why our family started the IBC with properly structured whole life insurance years ago, after thorough research. Regardless of your age or health, there is often a way to start the IBC. It's essential that you connect with a licensed insurance professional who specializes in and practices this powerful financial vehicle.

To Legacy!

Real Estate: Once you have some long-term investments going, I think then you have to start thinking about cash flow. What is an investment other than your business that, when you invest your money in, gives you money back each month, and your asset still grows? Meaning what you purchased is still going up in value so that someday when you sell it, you will get all your money back with additional value. This is where real estate can be a good fit. There are so many ways to do real estate. Some people flip houses, buy and hold single-family homes, or invest in large apartment buildings, referred to more as "multi-family." This is something that I am just now learning more about and getting into. I have traditionally invested heavily in myself and my businesses until the last year or so. I am glad that I made that a priority. However, I personally wish I had started investing at least a couple hundred dollars a month into that "set-it and forget-it account" and started to learn more about multi-family real estate early on. Once again, it goes back to whatever you do, just do something. Don't sit on the sideline. Decide what it is that you enjoy, that you find yourself thinking about a lot, and get in the game. If you don't know how to flip houses, manage apartment buildings, or all that, it's okay. You can learn, or there are many people who already know how, and you can simply invest your money with them. They find the deals, manage the deals, and you just become a financial investor. Many of these deals have an Average Rate of Return of 20% or higher. If you're not into real estate, then you can always go further in the stock market's direction. You can get started by setting up an account with Vanguard and starting by putting money into a Roth IRA today. Vanguard has very low fees, especially when you invest in Index Funds, and you can just set up a monthly investment amount that works for your budget. Once again, many people have had success with this over time. I am more geared towards Whole Life and Real Estate.

Cash and Risky Investments like Crypto- My last recommendation would be to Save some Cash with the intention of investing it. I know this sounds contradictory to what I just said when I said, just get in the game. What I mean is once you get some investments going, it is still a good idea to stack some cash. Being able to take advantage of a good deal from time to time can be a good thing. Plus, personally, I just like the feeling of having some money in the bank. One of the things that I am currently investing in is cryptocurrency. At the time of my writing of this book, inflation is higher than ever, interest rates are beginning to climb, and the government in the last two years has printed more money in the last two years than in the last 50 years combined. The world's financial system is broken in many ways, and I believe that Crypto has a lot of benefits that can give people options.

In my opinion, one of the things that you should look for in investing is what has the potential to give you a great ROI. The things above that I have mentioned, like the whole life policy, have guarantees, so those are safe. So, depending on your age and where you're at in life, you can be a little riskier. At this point in 2022, Crypto is still considered risky by many. However, I see it as an investment that has huge upside potential and serves a great purpose. People ask me all the time where I should start. I would just recommend starting with downloading the Coinbase app and learning all you can about Crypto. I personally invest in Bitcoin, Ethereum, Solano, Cardano, and some other coins. So far, these are the ones that have made sense to me. Once again, I'm not a professional financial advisor. I am just sharing what I do and what makes sense to me. If you're not a big Crypto fan, that's okay. The bottom line is that you save some money, look to invest in something, and make sure that it grows your money.

I have heard it said many times that **you don't earn your way to wealth; you invest it.** So no matter what you do, my friend, do something! You have the opportunity to change your family's financial legacy forever. It may start with you as it did for me. All I know is that I am glad that I got started, and I will never look back!

LET'S HAVE SOME FUN!

Okay, before I wrap up this Financial section, I feel compelled to talk about having some fun here real quick. What's the point of making a bunch of money, investing for the future, and then being miserable for the next 30 years until you retire? I see some people who are so focused on investing for the future that they forget to live life today! I believe in balance, my friends. As I mentioned earlier in this book, **Success without Fulfillment is the Ultimate failure.** If you make a bunch of money but don't enjoy your life, that makes no sense. So, one thing I have learned from my own mistakes is to get out and live life!

You must decide today what the things are that you want to spend your money on. Or the way I like to look at it, the things you want to invest your money in. What brings you joy and fulfillment? What makes you laugh? What are the things that you like to do as time just flies by? These should be the things that you are putting on your calendar more often and investing in.

For me and my wife we love to vacation! We love to golf! We love to go to concerts! We love to go to sporting events with our kids! We love to go out to eat at nice restaurants! We love to drive nice cars! As you know all these things above cost money. Also all these things are things that we can work towards that give us joy and fulfillment. There is nothing wrong with treating you and your family to a nice vacation once a year and going all out. This is an Investment in your family by the way if I haven't already mentioned that.

My point to all this is: Have Fun! Don't just make a bunch of money and be miserable. Live life to the fullest. Spend or, as I like to say, invest your money in creating magic moments that you will remember for a lifetime. I will never forget the cruise that we were able to take my momma on, the trip to Aruba with our kids, or the look on my wife's face when I surprised her with a Range Rover for her 50th birthday.

As I think back over the years of my life, I can tell you that I am so thankful that I had people early on that had the wealth to teach me the importance of having fun! Rachel and I set a goal to travel to beautiful places when we didn't have two nickels to rub together. That vision inspires us to work hard. In fact, as I write this sentence, we are on a plane to Cancun, Mexico, one of our favorite vacation spots, for the second time this month! **Your Vision will become your View,** my friends. So decide where you want to go, what you want to do, and Do it! Have some fun with your friends, enjoy the fruit of your labor, and never stop creating those magic moments for you and your family!

CHAPTER 12

THE CHAMPION LIFE CHALLENGE

As I begin the final chapter of this book, I want to say Congratulations! If you made it this far, I know you're 100% committed to being the Champion leader God created you to be. There is a country song by Eric Church called "Hell of a View" that I love. One of the lyrics in the song says, "This ain't for everybody." Meaning this Hell of a View isn't for everybody. It is, but it isn't. Every time I am sitting on a beautiful beach somewhere, I think about the people that will never see the beauty I am taking in because they feel it isn't for them. They believe they can't afford a nice vacation, so they never go on one. Whether it's a nice vacation, a loving marriage, or a thriving business, It is possible, but many people will never see this because of doubt.

If you have read this far and begun to put the principles that we have discussed into place, then I know your life is either changing or about to. My wife always says, "Your Vision Becomes Your View! As I have said before, **the best way to predict your future is to create it.** Many people just don't know how to create a vision worth viewing. Well, the good news is that you now know how! We have already covered that, and if you haven't already written out your vision, I encourage you to do so now, my friend! It will lay the foundation of what you focus on daily, what you pray about daily to ask God to help you create, and give you the drive to keep going even when you want to give up. The climb becomes worth it because, well, when you get to the top of the mountain, it's a hell of a view!

ONE DAY AT SUBWAY

As we near the end together, friends, I wanted to share one last story with you. This story is why this book that I hope has impacted your life so far even exists. I hope that It will encourage you. I hope that it will help you to decide to be the Champion God created you to be, and live your Champion Life. Even more important than that, is that It will inspire you to go and pay it forward. Meaning go help somebody else go to the next level in their life. That is what Champions do!

Throughout this book I have mentioned a man by the name of Jay multiple times. I have called him my mentor, friend, and I even sometimes call him Uncle Jay! He was the one that came into my life and Championed me to another level and I wanted to share the story with you, while also honoring him with this part of the book. See the Curt Tucker that I am today, doesn't exist without Jay Meyer and I am grateful for him in so many ways.

I remember it like it was yesterday. That time of my life in 2010 as I have already told you about was crazy. After losing everything through bankruptcy, being on the edge of a divorce, and trying to rebuild my life, I was more committed than ever to change. There is a saying, when the student is ready, the teacher will appear. So many of the things that I have covered in this book were taught to me by this teacher. My mentor, my friend, my Uncle Jay. So as it goes, One day at Subway, I walked in to grab a quick lunch in between training clients. There in the line before me stood a man I knew from church. He didn't know me, but I knew of him. He was a very influential man in our church. I knew part of his story from going to church over the years. He was very successful in business, married for many years, both kids played college basketball, and was very well respected as a leader within our church.

So as we were standing in line, inching closer and closer to ordering, something was telling me to introduce myself. I remember the conversation in my head at the time. The fear thought don't do it, you're not good enough or worthy of him helping you, he is probably way too busy for you. As we were almost ready to order, I did it! I reached out and tapped him on the shoulder. He turned around and I said. Hi my name is Curt Tucker. You don't know me, but I know you. **That one act of COURAGE my friends, absolutely changed the course of my life, my family's life, and I believe it will be a part of helping millions of others.**

I introduced myself, let him know that we went to the same church, and asked him if he would be open to doing lunch sometime. He immediately said of course and we exchanged information. After a couple months, I had the courage again to send an email asking for that lunch opportunity. After that lunch, I followed up with another email, asking Jay to personally coach me. I was hungry for change, and I knew I needed a mentor. Somebody I could personally work with, who would hold me accountable, and show me what I needed to know and do to succeed. This led to us working together for 90 days. Within 90 days Jay had helped me do things like. Create a Vision Statement, Get clear on my Purpose, and Create the right Priorities that I needed at the time. He helped me remove people, places, and things that weren't serving me. I was able to remove lies that had been holding me back for years. Those 90 days of my life that Jay and I worked closely together, was truly the foundational phase that my life today was built upon. Our friendship grew, eventually we became partners in a business for an awesome season of life, and my life has never been the same since.

I am so grateful for that season of my life, and for what Jay did for me. My life and My family for generations will be forever changed, because this man decided to be a Champion for Christ, and come alongside me, to help me become the Champion God created me to be. So I want to say right here, right now. Jay, thank you my friend for all that you have done for me, my family, and many others. Your investment in me, will be multiplied for the Kingdom, for many years to come. I love you my friend, and I am forever grateful for you! I promise I will continue to pay it forward, doing for others what you have done for me. This book is a major part of that mission!

MY CHALLENGE FOR YOU

So I want to close this book by giving you a challenge! Now that you have made the decision to become the Champion God has created you to be, and live the Champion Life. You have a Playbook to follow, and I can promise you if you commit daily to implementing these strategies and tactics, things will change faster than you think...My challenge to you is this: Go champion someone else! Remember the definition of a champion, my friend. Here it is, as a reminder. It has a dual meaning. It means to defeat or surpass all rivals in a competition, as well as to fight on behalf of someone else or to be a defender of Purpose. Man, I love that! **I feel so honored each day to be able to fight for people, helping them live this Champion Life** experiencing victory in every area. I am also so thankful that early in my journey, I had people that came alongside me and acted as champions when I didn't deserve it or even know what a Champion meant.

As I told you, I have a vision in my life to impact over a million men, and what I have learned is that it really starts with one. It starts with you! When you become the Champion God created you to be, you begin to look for Who God is calling you to Champion. The number of people you impact can multiply quickly. What you do matters, my friend. It starts by just pouring into one person, then another, and then, before you know it, the impact begins to snowball. God is into multiplying things! Here is a powerful illustration of how, when you decide and commit to leading yourself and begin to be a Champion for someone else, just how quickly the numbers can multiply. If you would be willing first to become the Champion God created you to be, Champion 10 people directly in your lifetime and encourage them to do the same, this very quickly becomes a million people. Generations forever changed because you made the decision to go ALL IN!

The POWER of ONE

& how it can impact MILLIONS

All leadership begins with self leadership

1 -It starts with me
10
100
1,000
10,000
100,000
1,000,000 millions impacted

Do YOU have the COURAGE to accept the challenge?

Who can I CHAMPION today?

CHAMPION BUILDERS ACADEMY
LIFE, LEADERSHIP, & BUSINESS COACHING

THE TIME IS NOW FOR YOU TO BEGIN AND WIN

My friend, I believe today is your day to begin a new journey. The possibilities for your life are endless. The plan that God has for your life is greater than you could ever think, hope, or imagine. All things really are possible to those who believe. So now it is up to you! I am inviting you on a journey. I truly want you to know that God wants you to Win, I want you to Win, and that you were created to Win. It won't be easy, but it will be worth it.

So can I encourage you today, my friend, to know that today is your day. You were created to be A Champion for Christ. I hope that you will implement what you have learned from my Successes and Messes, Trials and Errors, and Life Experience into your life to create the Champion life God has for you. I am not perfect in any way. I don't have all the answers, but I do know that I was called to write this book and that you were supposed to read it. My prayer is that you will partner with me in this movement to build Champions for Christ and help people live the Champion life.

It has been an honor spending this time with you, my friend. I hope to get the chance to meet you someday and hopefully hear a story or two about how this book has positively impacted your life. Your Champion Life is ready for you! Go and play full out, my friend. Never give up, Keep your Vision in front of you, and ask God daily to lead you into Becoming the Champion He created you to Be!

GET CONNECTED WITH CURT & JOIN THE CHAMPION MOVEMENT

Facebook- @curttucker
Instagram- @curtdtucker
Youtube-@curttucker
www.curtdtucker.com–Website
www.championlifemovement.com–Free FB Group and Community